Anglicanism: A Very Short Introduction

Very Short Introductions available now:

For more information visit our web site:
www.oup.co.uk/general/vsi/

Mark Chapman

ANGLICANISM

A Very Short Introduction

OXFORD
UNIVERSITY PRESS

OXFORD
UNIVERSITY PRESS

Great Clarendon Street, Oxford OX2 6DP

Oxford University Press is a department of the University of Oxford.
It furthers the University's objective of excellence in research, scholarship,
and education by publishing worldwide in

Oxford New York

Auckland Cape Town Dar es Salaam Hong Kong Karachi
Kuala Lumpur Madrid Melbourne Mexico City Nairobi
New Delhi Shanghai Taipei Toronto

With offices in

Argentina Austria Brazil Chile Czech Republic France Greece
Guatemala Hungary Italy Japan Poland Portugal Singapore
South Korea Switzerland Thailand Turkey Ukraine Vietnam

Oxford is a registered trade mark of Oxford University Press
in the UK and in certain other countries

Published in the United States
by Oxford University Press Inc., New York

© Mark Chapman 2006

The moral rights of the author have been asserted
Database right Oxford University Press (maker)

First published as a Very Short Introduction 2006

British Library Cataloguing in Publication Data

Data available

Library of Congress Cataloging in Publication Data

Chapman, Mark D. (Mark David), 1960–
Anglicanism : a very short introduction / Mark Chapman.
Includes bibliographical references and index.
ISBN-13: 978–0–19–280693–2 (alk. paper)
ISBN-10: 0–19–280693–9 (alk. paper)
1. Anglican Communion. I. Title.
BX5005.C35 2006
283—dc22   2006005507

ISBN 978–0–19–280693–2

7 9 10 8

Typeset by RefineCatch Ltd, Bungay, Suffolk
Printed in Great Britain by
Ashford Colour Press Ltd.

Contents

Acknowledgements

I am grateful to the many people who have helped me with this project – in particular, a number of friends have given freely of their time to read through the entire manuscript, helping me correct errors of fact and interpretation. By name I should mention Canon Dr Judith Maltby, the Revd Dr Peter Doll, the Revd Dr Andrew Atherstone, and my colleague, Canon Prof. Martyn Percy. I would also like to thank my students at Cuddesdon who have encouraged me for many years to think that I have something worth saying about Anglicanism. It is to them that this book is affectionately dedicated.

List of illustrations

The publisher and the author apologize for any errors or omissions in the above list. If contacted they will be pleased to rectify these at the earliest opportunity.

Chapter 1
The problems of Anglicanism

A national church

In 1904 Randall Davidson, Archbishop of Canterbury, visited the
United States to attend the General Convention of the Protestant
Episcopal Church. What he probably did not know was that among
the congregation when he preached at Trinity Church in Boston was
the great German theologian and sociologist Ernst Troeltsch.
Davidson's sermon made a lasting impact, as Troeltsch recalled in a
work published in 1921. Troeltsch, who pioneered the study of
religious organizations with his typology of church and sect, was
aware of what he called a 'glaring deficiency' in all his works: he had
never studied the Church of England in any depth. This was a pity,
since the Church of England might have provided him with a great
deal of support for the thesis he developed in his magisterial work,
The Social Teachings of the Christian Churches and Groups. The
Church of England can be understood as perhaps the purest form of
the late medieval church ideal surviving after the Reformation.
Indeed, an imaginative presentation of the Tudor Church could
have provided Troeltsch with evidence of a rather eccentric Western
example of something approaching a Byzantine state church.
Henry's VIII's vision of power and authority was not too far
removed from that of the Eastern emperors.

While it will become apparent through the course of this book that there is much more to Anglicanism than the English state church, it is nevertheless crucial to see the roots of today's global phenomenon in a Reformation which was experienced, as the historian Christopher Haigh puts it, 'as obedience, rather than conversion'. Most people 'obeyed the monarch's new laws rather than swallowed a preacher's new message'. However much doctrinal and liturgical innovation there might have been in the last 70 years of the 16th century, what was perhaps most important in shaping the Church of England was a vision of a Christian nation upheld by a Christian monarch. Uniformity and obedience were at the heart of the settlement. The Church of England owes as much to what one early 20th-century commentator called the 'absurd theory' of the Divine Right of Kings as to anything else. It was simple: kings had a right to rule over both their spiritual and temporal realm and no foreign potentate could usurp this power.

In the last 300 years or so, the Divine Right has mutated beyond recognition. While it is still very much a part of the British Constitution, in that governments still act on the basis of the prerogatives of the Crown, it is unthinkable that anybody could or would seek to impose a unified national religion. As the state changed, so the Church of England has had to mutate to have any chance of survival. The advantages it might have retained in aligning itself with the political classes through the 18th and 19th centuries were modest compared with the difficulties it began to experience as England opened up to a whole range of competing denominations and religions, not to mention the all-pervasive secularism of modern society.

The Church of England became a voluntary organization in which there was no longer any sense of external compulsion; it changed from being *the* religion of the English to being simply one denomination among others, though always one with certain privileges. Compulsory membership of the Church of England (apart from monarchs and their spouses) was finally abolished with the removal in 1871 of the religious tests on those attending Oxford and Cambridge universities. Consequently, the history of the Church of England from the 18th century is the search for an alternative locus of authority after the breakdown of the Divine Right of Kings. Some looked for authority in the direct experience of God in the heart or in God's Word as set forth in Scripture (the Evangelicals). Others sought it in God's appointed messengers, the bishops (the Anglo-Catholics).

That is the story of the Church of England which forms the subject of a significant part of this book. But what is obvious is that the Church of England is not the same thing as 'Anglicanism'. Anglicanism exists across the world in many different forms. The kind of independence from the state which was forced on a reluctant Church of England by various acts of parliament was embraced enthusiastically elsewhere. The American Protestant Episcopal Church, which was constitutionally forced to sever links with government during the American Revolution, had to learn to survive in the emerging democracy of the United States. Where there was no King there could be no Church of England. But could there be something else which resembled it? If the authority of the Church of England was derived from the divinely anointed King in Parliament, then what would replace it when that form of authority had been challenged or completely cast aside?

One of the most important problems in Anglicanism continues to be the search for authority. Some overseas churches tried out something like the English model with a unified vision of church and state under political control; but hardly any of these worked. For these churches, and for those many churches in the Anglican Communion that never enjoyed the benefits of establishment, there was a need to locate an alternative source of authority. While churches might have owed their origins to the Church of England, they were forced by their particular political circumstances to adopt new constitutions and forms of authority. Many began to enjoy the benefits of independence. In this way, Anglicanism became very different from the Church of England.

Some definitions

Church of England: The two historic provinces of Canterbury and York, with their origins at least as far back as St Augustine's mission of 597. Until the disestablishment of the Church in Wales in 1920, the Church of England also included the four ancient Welsh dioceses.

Anglican: The Latin term 'Ecclesia Anglicana' was used from the earliest days simply to describe the English Church: it appears in the 1215 Magna Carta and the 1534 Act of Supremacy. But, with one or two 17th-century exceptions, 'anglican' seems to have been first used in the mid-19th century to describe the Church of England in its independence from the Roman Catholic Church. Gladstone uses it in his *Church Principles* of 1840 when he talks about the validity of Anglican orders.

Anglicanism: This term was used by J. H. Newman in 1838 in distinction to 'Protestantism'. Later, he wrote: 'Anglicanism claimed to hold that the Church of England was nothing else than a continuation in this country of that one Church of which in old times Athanasius and Augustine were members.' Sometimes the term was equivalent to Anglo-Catholicism or English Catholicism. More recently, it has simply been used to indicate that type of Christianity which owes its origins to the Church of England (and sometimes also the American Episcopal Church).

Anglican Communion: The name given to the collection of 'particular or national churches' throughout the world, most of them owing their origins to the Church of England, and all in communion with the Archbishop of Canterbury. Although it might be dated from the separation of the American Episcopal Church from the Church of England, the term was not used before the 1850s, when the first colonial churches became independent provinces. The 'Communion' began to develop some form of organization from the first Lambeth Conference of 1867. Some churches (like the Spanish Reformed Church) have 'joined' the Communion, without ever having been Anglican.

Anglicanism and 'Europeanism'

Despite the changed relations to political power, there is still a crucial legacy of the old order: the idea of a national church acting independently of others has remained at the heart of Anglicanism. However, where the old colonial ties and a shared history and linguistic identity no longer bind churches together this means insuperable tensions are likely to emerge. Troeltsch's national church model might have suited the Church of England as it developed from Henry VIII to Charles II, but what has emerged since is quite different and far less amenable to such straightforward typologies. It is interesting that late in life Troeltsch himself recognized the difficulties of trying to write universal history: history was always written from a perspective. Trying to analyse Anglicanism in the 21st century is equally problematic. Where some have tried to locate the identity of Anglicanism in the historic formularies or liturgy of the Church of England and sought to impose these on worldwide Anglican churches through a commitment to a doctrinal minimum, others have seen this as a way of stifling the development of local churches in relation to their very different contexts.

The very idea of a global church raises enormous questions of power and authority. Here again Troeltsch is useful. He became the first theorist of a phenomenon he called Europeanism, a term which included both Europe and those places inhabited by European settlers across the world (including North America and Australia). For Troeltsch, Europe was simply one culture among many others: it did not determine truth across the world. Through history, however, many Europeans have failed to recognize these boundaries. A good early example is Samuel Purchas, the Jacobean adventurer and London rector. In his extraordinary account of overseas expansion (*His Pilgrimes. Or Relations of the World and the Religions observed in All Ages and Places Discovered, from the Creation unto this Present*), Purchas recognized that not only was Europe's religion superior, it was also the sole home of the 'Arts and Inventions'. Europe alone had given birth to 'the many artificial Mazes and Labyrinths in our watches'; similarly, in the arts of cooking, horse management, chemistry, gun-making, and 'innumerable other Mathematicall and Chymicall devises' Europe was pre-eminent. Most important, however, was the fact that

> God gives opportunitie by Navigation into all parts, that in the Sun-set and Evening of the World, the Sunne of righteousness might arise out of the West to illuminate the East, and fill both Hemispheres with his brighteness: that what the Apostles, by extraordinary dispensation sent, by extraordinary providence protected and conducted into all parts, by extraordinary gift of Tongues were able to preach to all sorts of men; this latter Age following those glorious Fathers and Founders . . . might attempt and in some sort attaine by helpes of these two Arts, Printing and Navigation, that Christ may be salvation to the ends of the Earth, and all nations may serve him; that according to the Scripture innumerable numbers of all Nations and Kindreds and peoples, and Tongues may be clothed with the white robes of the Lambe.

By using the great achievements of European culture, according to Purchas, overseas expansion might spread the message of an 'almost wholly and onely European' Jesus Christ 'who hath long since given a Bill of Divorce to ingratefull Asia where hee was borne, and Africa the place of his flight and refuge'. While most were rather less blunt in their perceptions of European superiority, such an attitude survived intact through the great period of colonial expansion in the 19th century. It was through Europeans that God acted, and it was through Europeans, endowed with the responsibility for divine mission, that civilization was carried to the rest of the world. The colonies, even those with established cultures and religions, were defined in relation to the European motherland.

Another historical example comes from the end of the 19th century. There were merely two black faces among the assembled bishops of the Anglican Communion who made their way to Glastonbury in 1897 after the fourth Lambeth Conference (Figure 1). The 1300th anniversary of the sending of St Augustine to Canterbury by Pope Gregory the Great was marked by a procession to the shrine at Glastonbury. Here, Joseph of Arimathea had purportedly planted the Holy Grail when he had supposedly brought Christianity to England's green and pleasant land. It is difficult to overlook the national myth. In celebrating a pre-Latinized form of Christianity, the bishops were giving credence to the great national myths of the 19th century. Although the Arthurian legends of Glastonbury are difficult to square with the more commonly held myths about the beginnings of English history in the Teutonic invasions, one thing is clear: the English Church and the Communion it spawned played their part in the national myths of English supremacy. However much the churches through the Empire might have connected with the local populations – and many of them became increasingly independent of English control – they were still primarily churches dominated by 'European' concerns and with a European leadership promoting European myths.

1. **Procession of Anglican bishops at Glastonbury, 1897**

Global expansion

When Davidson visited Boston in 1904, Anglicanism across the
world was a phenomenon dominated by white male Europeans and
settlers of European origins. The British Empire, the largest the
world had ever known, covered 11,000,000 square miles. The
English Church had spread out into the colonies and the new
self-governing dominions. 'Anglicanism' developed as the churches
in different parts of the world developed new ways of co-existing
with the political authorities, sometimes quite different from the
model provided by the settlement in the mother country (see
Chapter 6). Nevertheless, these churches were still primarily
European and transferred a way of looking at the world and of

understanding God through European eyes. Almost all of the higher clergy were European or American. Whether one marks the beginning of the Anglican Communion with the first English chaplains serving abroad from the 17th century, the consecration of Samuel Seabury in 1784 as the first bishop for the United States, or the first Lambeth Conference in 1867, it is clear that at the end of the 19th century Anglicanism was still primarily an English (and to some extent a North American) phenomenon.

Yet in the last 50 years or so, Anglicanism has changed beyond recognition. While the Church of England might still claim to be the largest of the Anglican churches, with stated figures of 26,000,000, this is little more than wishful thinking. There is no such thing as membership of the Church of England – fewer than a million attend church regularly and a similar number are registered on the electoral rolls of parish churches. Elsewhere, the situation is quite different: while no doubt figures might be exaggerated, Kenya claims 2,000,000 active members; Uganda 8,000,000; and Nigeria a staggering 17,500,000. The only 'European' churches to come close to resembling these figures are in Australia, with about 4,000,000, and the USA, with about 2,500,000, although again it is not clear precisely who is being included. What is clear is that something profound is happening to Anglicanism on a global level.

It is possible to see Anglicanism as a kind of global brand with a quality control office based in Lambeth, the home of the Archbishop of Canterbury. Just as transnational companies like Nike or Dell have shifted production across the globe but have retained control over the design of the product in developed countries, so Anglicanism's centres of productivity have shifted away from the old heartlands. When the old product seemed relevant and the global market seemed open, then the centres of power could continue much as they were. Missionaries could convey their products from north to south (or in the American case from east to west to east). This might lie behind some of the clamouring after an 'Anglican identity' in many parts of the world. A global market requires a consistent and reliable commodity: in Anglicanism's case, and according to one of the most popular versions of Anglican identity, this might be a *via media* between too much of one thing (Protestantism) and too much of the other (Catholicism).

But at this point the analogy with global markets breaks down: where the economic control of the multinationals keeps power away from the third-world workers, Anglican churches are different. The reason for this is partly historical. To defend their separation from Rome, the founding fathers of the Church of England relied on a doctrine of provincial autonomy: the Church of England was beholden to nobody but the King, least of all a bishop of some foreign land. Independence rather than 'communion' was at the heart of the Reformation. To plant that doctrine across the world, however, has created a situation which contains the seeds for its own destruction. When independent churches start asserting an identity which is no longer dependent on those who first sowed the seeds (as did Henry VIII four centuries beforehand when he separated from Pope Gregory's successors), then something has to give. And when that independent identity was tied up with that of a colonial power, matters are made more complex. To understand Anglicanism is to wrestle with globalization, with ecclesiastical and political independence, but also with post-colonialism.

Anglicanism and post-colonialism

It did not take long before the colonial churches themselves began to reflect on their situation, often in conscious dialogue with the colonizer. Gradually, as both colonizer and colonized questioned the legitimacy of the whole European imperialist and missionary enterprise, movements developed within the colonies attempting to rediscover an independent history. This meant that the English and North American model is not there to be envied or copied but is to be left behind. As the anti-colonialist Frantz Fanon put it in a North African context: 'We today can do everything, so long as we do not imitate Europe'. The mark of post-colonial maturity required the simultaneous acceptance of one's own cultural heritage and an openness to the heritage of others. Only by emphasizing the unique could the universal aspects of humanity be recognized, not in an inevitably Eurocentric universalism but through an ecumenism of uniqueness: there was no longer a centre. It was this sense of mutual recognition and exchange of ideas that characterized the post-colonial 'coming of age'.

Things had changed completely from the mid-19th century, when the whole task was to 'civilize' and 'educate'. As Samuel Wilberforce, Bishop of Oxford, remarked in 1853, the vocation of the British people was

> to leave as the impress of their intercourse with inferior nations, marks of moral teaching and religious training, to have made a nation of children see what it was to be men – to have trained mankind in the habits of truth, morality and justice, instead of leaving them in the imbecility of falsehood and perpetual childhood; and above all, to have been instrumental in communicating to them, not by fierce aggression and superior power – but by gentle persuasion, that moral superiority, that greatest gift bestowed by God upon ourselves, true faith in His word and true belief in the revelation of His Son.

When the 'children' grow up, however, they might have much to teach their educators.

Through the 20th century many became conscious of the effects of colonialism on the churches. As early as 1912, for instance, William Temple, who became one of the greatest of the modern archbishops of Canterbury, noted that the church would change through its contact with different cultures. Unity did not imply uniformity, but was instead a 'socialist' unity, 'where the single life of the whole absolutely depends on the diversity of the parts alike in form and function'. While recognizing that England had shaped his understanding of Christ, to go further and suppose that English

Christianity expressed the goal of the divine mission would be to universalize one particular expression of the fallen condition of humanity. In any society the 'Church cannot be more than a limited distance ahead of the society in which its members live'. The conversion of the colonies had nothing to do with the conversion of indigenous peoples to the English civic virtues. Temple asked presciently, if somewhat patronizingly:

> What will be the result when the mystical and spiritual nations of the east, and the affectionate and childlike peoples of Africa, are quickened by contact with the perfection of their own virtues in the Person of Jesus of Nazareth?

For Anglicanism, the parody of Tertullian by the black American theologian Robert E. Hood is highly relevant: 'Is Greek metaphysics still relevant? What do Athens and Rome have to do with Egypt, Ethiopia, West Africa, East Africa and South Africa? Likewise, what do Wittenberg, Geneva, Zürich, Canterbury, Edinburgh, Richmond (Virginia), and New York have to do with sub-Saharan Africa and the Afro-Caribbean come of age?' A more specifically Anglican question might be: 'What has Canterbury (or New York City) to do with Hong Kong, Lagos, Mombasa, or Tamil Nadu?' Many theologians have questioned the validity of the metaphysical and universalizing assumptions of European Christianity when they are transferred to the African context. As long ago as 1970, the Kenyan Anglican John Mbiti noted that in Africa the 'search after [the Supreme Being's] attention is utilitarian and not purely spiritual; it is practical and not mystical. . . . [Africans] do not seem to search for him as the final reward or satisfaction of the human spirit.' Different churches across the globe can develop very different ways of thinking about God and his relations with the world. With its history of autonomous action and its absence of central authority, except at a very rudimentary level, Anglicanism has always been particularly prone to ever-increasing diversity. Showing how and why this has come to be and whether Anglicanism has a future is the purpose of this Very Short Introduction.

Chapter 2
Establishing the church

The Reformation: did it really happen?

The Cambridge Camden Society was one of the most successful undergraduate societies of all time. It was established by two earnest Cambridge undergraduates, J. M. Neale and Benjamin Webb, in 1839. Its aims are instructive:

> Church Building at home and in the Colonies; Church Restoration in England and abroad; the theory and practice of ecclesiological architecture; the investigation of Church Antiquities; the connection of Architecture with Ritual; the science of Symbolism: the principles of Church Arrangement; Church Musick and all the Decorative Arts.

The success of this society and other like-minded groups was extraordinary: there are only about 100 of the 7,000 or so medieval churches in the whole of England that were not restored or rebuilt between about 1840 and 1900. In the same period many thousands of new churches were built, nearly all in a medieval Gothic style.

The same was true throughout the world: mission huts prefabricated in Norwich with 14th-century features were sent to far-flung parts of the Empire. Until very recently, to walk into Anglican churches throughout the world was to enter a Victorian vision of what the medieval world might have been like. The many changes to church buildings seen in the 16th and 17th centuries were literally cleared away. At least architecturally, it was as if the Reformation had not really happened. Many Victorians would have preferred it that way. Historians and theologians, particularly at Oxford, contributed to what the historian Diarmaid MacCulloch has called the 'the myth of the English Reformation' – that it did not happen.

While this might have been the founding myth of some expressions of Anglicanism, it could not be further from the truth: between the late 1520s and the end of the century, virtually everything about the Church of England changed: its theology, its ritual, its relationship with the state and with the people. Only its parish and diocesan structures remained largely intact. Although different aspects moved at varying speeds, and it is probably better to talk of reformations in the plural, it is undeniable that in the 16th century England experienced a thoroughgoing reformation. Victorians influenced by the Anglo-Catholic revival might have tried to rewrite history, but even they failed to remove the reformation from the Church of England.

Inventing Ecclesia Anglicana

The Church of England was reformed in a different way from many of its continental counterparts. At least at the beginning, the question of political authority came before theology: influenced by a group of advisers, including many church leaders, King Henry VIII came to believe that the Pope had usurped the authority which was rightfully his. The theory was simple: all authority both temporal and spiritual ultimately resided in the King under God. The circumstances surrounding the assertion of Royal Supremacy over the church are well known. The King desired a male heir and sought an annulment from Katharine of Aragon, the aunt of Charles V, the Holy Roman Emperor. These powers of annulment could only be exercised by the Pope. But given that he was at the mercy of Charles, there was little progress made, despite pleadings from Cardinal Wolsey, Archbishop of York. The Universities were asked to prepare a decent case to the Roman authorities and reaffirmed the Biblical injunction: 'it is so unlawful for a man to marry his brother's wife (Leviticus, 20:21) that the Pope hath no power to dispense therewith'. Since Katherine had been married to Henry's brother Arthur, this would have had the effect of nullifying his marriage.

It was in representing this case in Rome in 1529–1530 that Thomas Cranmer began his career in Henry's service, managing to obtain a number of 'censurae' (university opinions) in Henry's favour. At the same time, Henry's lawyers, in particular Thomas Cromwell, a friend of the Boleyn family, maintained that England had complete legal independence from Rome: a purely local decision would be sufficient to dispense with canon law. There was a general riffling through historical precedent, particularly the old statutes of praemunire which dated back to 1353, which asserted the illegality of appeals outside the realm of England. Various scholars assembled collections of texts emphasizing the King's rights over the English Church as well as the church's right to resist the Bishop of Rome. These provided the theory that was so thoroughly put into practice in the 1530s.

At the beginning of the 1530s, Henry began to assert his authority over the church. In January 1531, he accused the whole of his clergy of exercising a spiritual authority which was in direct contradiction with their duties as subjects. While this was primarily a tax-raising measure, in that he promised pardon in return for a fine of £118,000, the preamble to the grant of pardon reveals something of Henry's claims. He asked convocation (the church's parliament) to acknowledge him as 'sole protector and supreme head of the English Church'. After some controversy, Bishop John Fisher of Rochester added the clause 'as far as the law of Christ allows'. The King had been acknowledged as the 'singular protector, supreme lord' and even 'supreme head of the Church of England'.

Absolute power

In early 1532, Henry (Figure 2) sought an act of submission from the clergy to ensure that all ecclesiastical legislation would be subject to royal approval. Again, this was far from plain sailing. On 11 May, for instance, the King had to show the House of Commons a copy of the bishops' oath of allegiance with the commentary that 'they be but half our subjects, yea, and scarce our subjects'. Four

2. Henry VIII, creator of the independent English Church, in the late 1530s

days later he succeeded in obtaining their submission. By the end of the year, matters had become more urgent: Anne Boleyn was pregnant. She married Henry secretly in January 1533. Stephen Gardiner, Bishop of Winchester, pressed the King's case for annulment through convocation. On 23 May 1533, Thomas Cranmer, by now Archbishop of Canterbury, declared Henry's marriage to Katherine void, and on 28 May the marriage to Boleyn was declared lawful. There was (not surprisingly) a strong reaction from Rome; Convocation, however, declared that the Bishop of Rome had no more authority outside his province than any other bishop.

The period of the royal annulment was accompanied by a number of acts which asserted royal sovereignty over areas that had been traditionally the province of the church. Instead of the original plan simply forbidding appeals to Rome against a local decision on the divorce, Thomas Cromwell went significantly further in the Act in Restraint of Appeals of February 1533. His legislation included the momentous preamble claiming the unfettered or 'imperial' authority of the English Crown over matters both temporal and spiritual. This meant that under God the King commanded absolute obedience and total control over the church; and it must be said that according to such a theory God would find it hard to do very much without the royal assent. Everything over which the church had previously exercised authority (including marriage, testaments, and tithes) was to be 'finally and definitively adjudged and determined, within the king's jurisdiction and authority, and not elsewhere, in such courts spiritual and temporal of the same, as the natures, conditions, and qualities of the causes . . . shall require'. This meant that the King was absolute in his own domains and his courts could decide on matters both sacred and secular. The only exception to the King's authority was the power to consecrate bishops (although he appointed them) and to administer the sacraments. To all intents and purposes, the King had become the Pope of England.

Preamble to the Act in Restraint of Appeals

Where by divers sundry old authentic histories and chronicles, it is manifestly declared and expressed, that this realm of England is an Empire, and so hath been accepted in this world, governed by one supreme head and king, having the dignity and royal estate of the imperial crown of the same, unto whom a body politic, compact of all sorts and degrees of people, divided in terms, and by names of spiritualty and temporalty, be bounden and owe to bear, next to God, a natural and humble obedience ... The King, his most noble progenitors, and the nobility and commons of this said realm, at divers and sundry parliaments as well in the time of King Edward I, Edward III, Richard II, Henry IV, and other noble kings of this realm, made sundry ordinances, laws, statutes, and provisions for the entire and sure conservation of the prerogatives, liberties, and pre-eminences of the said imperial crown of this realm, and of the jurisdiction spiritual and temporal of the same, to keep it from the annoyance as well of the see of Rome, as from the authority of other foreign potentates, attempting the diminution or violation thereof, as often, from time to time, as any such annoyance or attempt be known or espied.

Crucial in developing the theory of absolute authority was the barrister Christopher St Germain (c.1460–1540), whose *Doctor and Student: Or Dialogues Between A Doctor of Divinity and a Student in the Laws of England* was published in English in 1531. He borrowed from the 14th-century defender of the Emperor, Marsilius of Padua, who claimed that the functions of priests were limited to the realms of piety, consecration, and sacrament (the *potestas ordinis*). All other areas (the *potestas jurisdictionis*) were placed under the secular authority. The logic of this thought led him to assert that the King was 'high sovereign over the people, which hath not only charge on the bodies but also on the souls of the subject'. The King thus had an 'absolute power as to possession of all temporal things within this realm . . . to take them from one man and to give them to another without any cause or consideration'.

Others shared similar ideas. In 1535, Stephen Gardiner defended the principle of royal supremacy in his book *De vera obedientia* (*On True Obedience*): an Englishman was the King's subject, not only as a citizen, but also as a Christian. God gives earthly care for human beings to the Monarch both in matters spiritual and temporal:

> All sorts of people are agreed upon this point with most steadfast consent, learned and unlearned, both men and women: that no manner of person born and brought up in England hath aught to do with Rome. All manner of people receiving and embracing the truth with one whole consent acknowledge, honour, and reverence the King for the Supreme Headship of the Church upon earth. They bid the Bishop of Rome farewell.

Even though Gardiner later retracted what he had said, the theory of Royal Supremacy turned out to be a very radical theory indeed. The assertion that all church property belonged ultimately to the King had far-reaching consequences.

The English Pope

The legislation asserting the King's authority over the church continued through the next few years. In 1534 the Dispensations Act ensured that there would be no more payments to Rome to dispense with canon law. Dispensations would be secured instead from the Archbishop. Under the Annates statutes, payments of first-fruits (that is, the first year's revenue from an ecclesiastical post which went to Rome) were transferred to the Crown as a means of clerical taxation. Statutes also ensured the election of bishops without papal interference. The coping-stone to this series of statutes was the Act of Supremacy of November 1534. The King was acknowledged as 'the only supreme head in earth of the Church of England, called *Anglicana Ecclesia*'. Moreover, the King (rather than the Archbishop) took over the right of visitation (inspection) of the monasteries and the clergy, 'to repress, redress, reform, order, correct, restrain, and amend all such errors, heresies, abuses, offences, contempts and enormities', both for the 'increase of virtue of Christ's religion' and for 'the conservation of the peace, unity and tranquillity of this realm'. The King was thus the chief patron of the English Church. His coffers were also considerably strengthened at the expense of the Pope and the English clergy.

On the basis of these great acts of state, Henry exercised what has been called his 'Caesaro-papalism' through the person of Thomas Cromwell, who, in his role as vicegerent, was given a precedence over the whole episcopate. He quickly ordered preaching in defence of the Royal Supremacy, and sheriffs and Justices of the Peace were instructed to keep an eye on bishops. The episcopate changed rapidly with no fewer than six supporters of Anne Boleyn appointed by 1535. The obvious material effect of the Royal Supremacy was that the King had the right to confiscate and redistribute the property of the church. While for Cranmer and Cromwell monasticism was a pious fraud, for Henry it was a useful source of revenue. Henry set about some degree of redistribution of ecclesiastical goods, including the foundation of the Regius Professorships at Oxford and Cambridge, the foundation of Trinity College, Cambridge, and the establishment of a number of new dioceses. The dissolution of the monasteries allowed the king to increase his revenue by about one third, making about £800,000 by 1547. Despite widespread unrest, particularly the Pilgrimage of Grace in 1536 and 1537 when 30,000 rose up against the religious changes, Cromwell's policy met with initial success.

The same period saw the beginnings of the reformation of doctrine. By 1536, there was a general suppression of some of the traditional practices: saints' days were reduced in number and clergy were enjoined not to 'set forth or extol any images, relics or miracles for any superstition or lucre, nor allure the people by any enticements to the pilgrimage of any saint'. Two years later clergy were instructed to take down images 'abused' by their association with pilgrimages or offerings. Although Henry had earlier proved himself an opponent of the continental reformation, the need for diplomatic alliance with German princes meant that it was expedient to show a degree of sympathy to Lutheran teaching. Thomas Cranmer set about preparing a statement of post-papal orthodoxy which was deeply influenced by German theologians.

Seeking compromise in Convocation, Henry was eventually able to reach agreement on the 'Ten Articles' in July 1536. These contain the seeds for subsequent doctrinal formulations and controversy. The first five articles concern 'things necessary to our salvation', and are based on the Bible and creeds as the norms of faith. The number of sacraments is restricted to penance, eucharist, and baptism (as in early Lutheranism). The articles affirmed the doctrine of the real presence of the Body and Blood of Christ 'under the form and figure of bread and wine'. The second five articles focus on 'such things as have been of a long continuance for a decent order and an honest policy . . . though they be not expressly commanded of God, nor necessary to our salvation'. Article VIII asserts, for instance, that while Christ is the only mediator, it is nevertheless laudable to pray to saints in heaven. Similarly, Article IX affirms that while the rites and ceremonies of Christ's Church do not 'have the power to remit sin', they nevertheless can 'stir up our minds unto God, by whom only our sins are forgiven'. While retaining faith in purgatory, Article X was explicitly anti-Roman:

it is a very good and a charitable deed to pray for souls departed

[but] it is much necessary that such abuses be clearly put away, which under the name of purgatory hath been advanced, as to make men believe that through the Bishop of Rome's pardons souls might clearly be delivered out of purgatory.

All in all, the bluntness of the Lutheran insistence on justification by faith was compromised by the retention of many of the traditional practices of the church, including services in Latin. Henry wanted a longer statement of doctrine, and Cranmer and Cromwell set about negotiating a treatise on doctrine, the *Institution of a Christian Man*, or *Bishops' Book*, in 1537. The King remained conservative, however, and it was not accepted as a doctrinal formulation, but merely as an exhortation to all clergy. It was given authorization only for a three-year period.

Several bishops, including Gardiner, Cuthbert Tunstall of Durham, and John Stokesley of London, together with Thomas Howard, Duke of Norfolk, grew increasingly anxious about the spread of Lutheran ideas. By 1538, external circumstances had changed and the King called a halt to theological experimentation. This was marked symbolically with the burning of John Lambert for denying the real presence of Christ in the eucharist. Henry was able to reassert his Catholic orthodoxy. Cranmer's advice in doctrinal matters was ignored, and on 16 May 1539, Howard asked the House of Lords to consider the six controversial issues of transubstantiation, communion in one kind, vows of chastity, 'votive' masses (offered up for a particular cause), clerical celibacy, and private confession. The Six Articles, the 'whip of six strings', amounted to a conservative restatement of doctrine: Article V, for instance, reaffirmed that 'it is meet and necessary that private masses be continued and admitted in this the King's English Church and congregation'. Nevertheless, there was no question of returning to the Pope.

Cromwell was denounced on the grounds of treason and heresy, and executed on 28 June 1540. Henry then married Katherine

Howard, a member of the conservative faction, ditching the
Bishops' Book. A new committee on doctrine then drew up the
so-called *King's Book* (1543), which moved further away from
Lutheranism:

> this word justification, as it is taken in scripture, signifieth the
> making of us righteous afore God. . . . And albeit God is the
> principal cause and chief worker of this justification in us, without
> whose grace no man can do no good thing . . . yet it so pleaseth the
> high wisdom of God, that man . . . shall be also a worker by his free
> consent and obedience . . . in the attaining of his own justification.

Liturgically there was remarkably little that was new in Henry's
time, although English Bibles had been placed in parish churches,
which meant that people could understand Scripture for the first
time. In 1544, Cranmer produced the first English liturgical text,
the Litany. Although it drew almost completely from existing texts,
its opposition to Rome was intense:

> From all sedycion and privey conspiracie, from the tyranny of the
> bisshop of Rome and all his detestable enormyties, from all false
> doctrine and heresye, from hardnes of hearte, and conmtempte of
> thy worde and commaundemente:
> *Good lorde deliver us.*

Henry died on 28 January 1547 a Catholic, albeit a very singular
one. He left £666 to the poor to pray for his soul: purgatory had still
not been abolished, at least not for kings. Henry's successor,
Edward, was still in his minority, which meant that a regency had to
be set up (Figure 3).

3. The infant King Edward VI is shown with his counsel, ensuring the Pope has no jurisdiction in England

Edward VI and the Protestant Reformation

On 31 January 1547, Edward Seymour, Duke of Somerset, was named as protector of the realm, exercising near-sovereign powers. This made possible a determined Protestant reformation. By July, new injunctions against images were issued. A Chantries Act dissolved some 4,000 charitable foundations and denounced the doctrine of purgatory. Most important was the first full-scale English-language liturgy in the first Book of Common Prayer of 1549. Almost all parishes had purchased their copies by June. When Somerset was replaced by John Dudley, Earl of Warwick, later Duke of Northumberland, this failed to halt reform.

In January 1550, Cranmer produced ordination services along the lines suggested by Martin Bucer (1491–1551), the Strasbourg reformer. Bucer was made Regius Professor at Cambridge and acted as theological consultant, along with his Italian counterpart at Oxford, Peter Martyr. Bucer began to lecture in defence of Zwingli, who denied the real presence of Christ in the eucharist; before long, several clergy were dismissed for preaching transubstantiation. Stone altars, which signified the offering up of masses on behalf of the dead, were denounced by Bishop Hooper in Gloucester, who even refused to wear the traditional vestments at his consecration. There was a campaign for the removal of altars in London under Ridley, and in Bath and Wells under Barlow. Altars were quickly dismantled across the country. It looks likely that the 1549 Prayer Book was intended as a temporary compromise and, before long, a second, significantly revised, book was introduced in November 1552. Equally important were the Forty-Two Articles of Religion which condemned in like manner the Romish and more anti-authoritarian teachings of the radical reformation. The Edwardian Reformation introduced a strongly reformed doctrine and liturgy which borrowed heavily from continental models. Had Edward not died prematurely, it is likely that the Reformation would have continued and the Church of England might have looked far more like Geneva or Zurich.

In this period of rapid change, it would be wrong to say that the people conceded to reforms willingly: for the most part, there was reluctant acquiescence. However, England was no democracy and few reformers had a high opinion of the will of the people. Hooper claimed, for instance, that the people, 'that many headed monster, is still wincing, partly through ignorance and partly fascinated by the inveiglements of the bishops and the malice and the impiety of the mass-priests'. Bucer was marginally more measured: 'Things are for the most part carried on by means of ordinances, which the majority obey very grudgingly, and by the removal of the instruments of the ancient superstition.' The picture that emerges is of a reforming episcopacy held in check by the threat of financial expropriation. They were assisted by an important group of educated preachers and academics imposing reformed doctrine on the mass of more or less superstitious Englishmen.

The Edwardian Prayer Books

1549: Cranmer sought to remove the complexity of the past so that everything was 'plain and easily' understood. Although he borrowed heavily from continental reformed service books, he also retained elements from the old Latin services, especially the Sarum (Salisbury) use. The 1549 Book was an interim rite that lasted merely three years. It was set to music by John Merbecke in a version which is still commonly used. The communion service (called 'The Supper of the Lord and Holy Communion, Commonly called the Mass') retained much from earlier missals. The bread was distributed with these words, indicating the real presence of Christ:

THE body of our Lord Jesus Christ which was given for thee, preserve thy body and soul unto everlasting life.

1552: Changes were made emphasizing the reformed character of the liturgy. There were long exhortations on human unworthiness at communion. The service was called simply 'The Order for the Administration of the Lord's Supper, or Holy Communion'. The Ten Commandments were introduced, and there was a new prayer of consecration. The exorcism and anointing were omitted from Baptism. Communion and prayers for the dead were removed from the Burial service. These smacked of the old religion in which the living could perform religious acts on behalf of the dead. At Communion the bread was distributed with very different words:

TAKE and eat this, in remembrance that Christ died for thee, and feed on him in thy heart by faith, with thanksgiving.

The 'Black Rubric' was added at the last moment and sought to assure people that kneeling at the Communion did not imply any sense of adoration of the bread and wine. Real presence was explicitly ruled out by the last two sentences:

Whereas it is ordained in the book of common prayer, in the administration of the Lord's Supper, that the Communicants kneeling should receive the holy Communion: which thing being well meant, for a signification of the humble and grateful acknowledging of the benefits of Christ, given unto the worthy receiver, and to avoid the profanation and disorder, which about the holy Communion might else ensue: Lest yet the same kneeling might be thought or taken otherwise, we do declare that it is not meant thereby, that any adoration is done, or ought to be done, either unto the Sacramental bread or wine there bodily received, or unto any real and essential presence there being of Christ's natural flesh and blood. For as concerning the Sacramental bread and wine, they remain still in their very natural substances, and therefore may not be adored, for that were Idolatry to be abhorred of all faithful Christians. And as concerning the natural body and blood of our saviour Christ, they are in heaven and not here. For it is against the truth of Christ's true natural body, to be in more places than in one, at one time.

Thomas Cranmer (1489–1556)

Crucial in the changes to English religion was Thomas Cranmer (Figure 4), one of the most complex figures of the Tudor period. Doctrinally it is quite clear that Cranmer's sympathies, at least from the mid-1530s, were broadly Protestant. He had, after all, married a niece of the wife of the German Reformer Osiander. And yet

4. Thomas Cranmer, Archbishop of Canterbury under Henry VIII and Edward VI, was the chief compiler of the Book of Common Prayer

Cranmer failed to initiate doctrinal reform in Henry's time after the King's change of opinion in the late 1530s. Not surprisingly, there are many pictures of Cranmer as the man who drifted with the tide, the 'teflon prelate', as the historian Patrick Collinson put it. In Edward's reign, his reformed credentials were clear. His homilies (sermons written to be read out by those who did not have a licence to preach) are expositions of a basically Lutheran Creed. He wrote in his *Homily of Salvation*:

> Justification is the office of God only, and is not a thing which we render unto him . . . yet we must renounce the merits of all our said virtues, of faith, hope, charities and all other good deeds, which we either have done, shall do, or can do, as things that be far too weak and insufficient and unperfect, to deserve remission of our sins and our justification.

Similarly, he was insistent that the bread and wine did not literally become Christ's body and blood as earlier theology had maintained, but rather they became *for us* his body and blood on the basis of our faith ('receptionism'). Similarly, his long-winded prayer of consecration, which amounts to a lecture on the Atonement, makes it clear that sacrifice is union with the one all-sufficient sacrifice of Christ and is nothing to do with us.

For somebody enthralled by the reformation like Cranmer, the doctrine of royal supremacy raised serious questions: in the end one had to accept the divinely appointed monarch's will. As a biographer put it:

> If the known facts of Cranmer's life are impartially examined, nearly all the apparent contradictions disappear and a consistent personality emerges. Like most of his contemporaries . . . Cranmer believed in Royal absolutism. He believed that his primary duty as a Christian was to strengthen the power of the King, and was prepared if necessary to sacrifice all his other doctrines to accomplish this.

Despite the reformation of doctrine, obedience to the sacred office of the King remained at the heart of English religion.

This doctrine was tested to its extreme following Edward's death.

After the failure to put the Protestant Lady Jane Grey on the throne, Mary succeeded with her husband, Philip II of Spain. Since they were Roman Catholics, this meant that the only temporal authority Cranmer acknowledged was turned against what he regarded as religious truth. Bishop Hugh Latimer's prediction of 1549 proved true:

> Oh what a plague were it, that a strange King, of a strange land, and a strange religion should rule over us . . . God keep such a king from us! Well, the King's grace hath sisters, my Lady Mary and my Lady Elizabeth, which by succession and course are inheritors to the crown, who, if they should marry with strangers, what should ensue? God knoweth.

The case of Cranmer shows the inevitable tension between the doctrine of Royal Supremacy and a Protestant faith where authority is established solely on the basis of Scripture. To recant or not to recant was Cranmer's problem; as is evident from the accounts of his inquisition in the University Church in Oxford, there was ambivalence to the very end. When he finally recanted, he did so, not in a point of doctrine, but in so far as he was content to submit himself to the laws of the King and Queen. However, in the end, Cranmer withdrew his recantation and denounced the Pope as antichrist, the chief enemy of Christ. Perhaps the inherent ambiguity of a reformed Church of England under the absolute authority of the monarch had finally occurred to him.

The Elizabethan settlement

Elizabeth succeeded to the throne on 17 November 1558. There was a rapid attempt to return to the situation before Mary's reign in 'matters and ceremonies of religion'. Within a few years nearly all the bishops had been replaced. Matthew Parker (1504–75) was appointed Archbishop of Canterbury in 1559. A revised Prayer Book was introduced which included some compromises that allowed it to pass through the still conservative House of Lords: there was a recognition that the Church of England stood between the poles of Rome and the more extreme varieties of Protestantism. It grew to be, as Bishop Simon Patrick put it over a century later, a 'virtuous mediocrity' between 'the meretricious gaudiness of the Church of Rome and the squalid sluttery of fanatic conventicles'.

The Elizabethan Prayer Book of 1559

Some changes were made. The 'Black Rubric' was dropped; the two different sentences of administration of the sacraments somewhat incoherently combined:

The Body of our Lord Jesus Christ which was given for thee, preserve thy body and soul into everlasting life [1549]; take and eat this in remembrance that Christ died for thee and feed on him in your hearts by faith with thanksgiving [1552].

Prayers against the Pope were dropped from the Litany; a new 'ornaments' rubric was added prescribing the use of traditional vestments – precisely what this meant remained a matter of heated debate for a long time to come.

The Morning and Evening prayer shall be used in the accustomed place of the church, chapel, or Chancel, except it shall be otherwise determined by the ordinary of the place: and the chancels shall remain, as they have done in times past.

And here is to be noted, that the Minister at the time of the communion, and at all other times in his ministration, shall use such ornaments in the church, as were in use by authority of parliament in the second year of the reign of King Edward VI. according to the act of parliament set in the beginning of this book.

In January 1559, Parliament conferred the title of Supreme Governor (rather than Supreme Head) on the Queen. The doctrine of royal supremacy, however, survived intact and it was soon put to use. Once again the suppression of heresy was put outside the church's direct control into the hands of the Ecclesiastical Commission, which was given the power to decide on heresy 'by the authority of the canonical scriptures, or by the first four General Councils'. A series of Injunctions was issued to bring the country into line with the Protestant liturgy. The Act of Uniformity imposed a fine of 12d on all those failing to attend church; some 300 clergy resigned or were dismissed from office. Many of the hastily restored shrines and altars were finally dismantled. In the next few years, more ecclesiastical lands were confiscated, which led to a general impoverishment of the church: Henry VIII's new diocese for Middlesex was reunited with London and its endowments seized by the Crown; many bishoprics were left vacant for long periods.

Defending the Church of England

It was Bishop John Jewel (1522–1571) (Figure 5) who offered the first full-scale theological justification for the Elizabethan settlement. Jewel made his mark in Oxford as an assistant to Peter Martyr and had gone into exile on the Continent in Mary's reign. Like other exiles, including John Foxe, Jewel was to shape the Church of England's understanding of itself decisively. Shortly after Elizabeth's succession he was made Bishop of Salisbury. Like Parker, who had written a book on the continuities of British history, he emphasized the Church of England's claim to antiquity. In a famous sermon, he challenged those who clung to Rome 'to bring any one sufficient sentence out of old Catholicke Doctor, or Father; or out of any old Generell Councell; or out of the Holy Scriptures of God' to justify their practices. Shortly afterwards, Jewel worked up his ideas into the *Apologia Ecclesiae Anglicanae* published in Latin in 1562 and soon translated into English, a book which gained the official seal of approval in the

5. John Jewel, Bishop of Salisbury, wrote the first justification of the Elizabethan settlement

reign of James I. Writing against a Roman Catholic, Jewel sought to show that the Church of England was neither one of the 'sundry sects', nor had it fallen into the immorality of the Roman Church. The first 600 years or so of Christian history, combined with the supremacy of Scripture, were his sources. In turn, he tried to show that the Church of Rome had 'forsaken the fellowship of the Holy Fathers'. He challenged the Pope: 'which of all the fathers have at any time called you by the name of the highest prelate, the universal bishop, or the head of the Church?'

Jewel addresses the crucial issue of the authority to reform doctrine. Against the charge that the Church of England had acted unilaterally and had failed to base its decisions on a council, he claimed:

> Yet truly we do not despise councils, assemblies, and conferences of bishops and learned men; neither have we done that we have done altogether without bishops or without a council. The matter hath been treated in open parliament, with long consultation, and before a notable synod and convocation.

For Jewel, Parliament (an all-male and quite unrepresentative body at the time) is understood as a legitimate council of the church, even more so because it is convened by the monarch, who alone has the authority to summon councils (as was asserted in Article XXI: 'General Councils may not be gathered together without the commandment and will of princes'). Jewel then goes on the offensive, criticizing the Council of Trent, which lacked this civil authority and could therefore not be regarded as a general council. Besides, he went on, 'Whatsoever it be, the truth of the gospel of Jesus Christ dependeth not upon the councils', since, as Article XXI asserted, all councils can err.

For Jewel, the Church of England was as near as it was possible to get 'to the Church of the Apostles and of the old catholic bishops and fathers'. The errors of the Church of Rome had been purged by returning to the Scriptures, 'the very sure and infallible rule, whereby may be tried whether the church doth stagger or err, and whereunto all ecclesiastical doctrine ought to be called to account'. In any dispute Scripture was supreme over the fathers, who may 'not be compared with the word of God'. The Fathers were 'the stars, fair and beautiful and bright; yet they are not the sun: they bear witness of the light, they are not the light'.

How this source of authority related to that of Parliament was more complex. The central issue was what happened when Scripture was silent. How then were decisions to be made? Jewel emphasized the importance of good order and decency:

> we keep still and esteem, not only those ceremonies which we are sure were delivered us from the apostles, but some others too besides, which we thought might be suffered without hurt to the church of God; because we had a desire that all things in the Holy Congregation might (as Paul Commandeth) 'be done with comeliness, and in good order'.

While some practices were not matters of faith ('things indifferent'), they were to be retained if they built up the congregation and brought order to the church. In this Jewel shared a method with many of the continental reformers, including both Luther and Calvin. What was less clear was who should decide on what should be included among these indifferent things. If the definitive interpreter of Scripture was the highest authority of the land, there was little scope for those who sought a greater role for the church to decide for itself.

Putting the settlement into practice: what to wear in church

Although at the beginning of Elizabeth's reign there were efforts to woo Catholics, by 1562 the Pope had forbidden them from attending the Church of England. By 1570, the Queen had been excommunicated. Where Jewel argued against Catholics, the next stage in the creation of an identity for the Church of England involved controversies with those at the other end of the spectrum, much of it focused on matters indifferent, including ecclesiastical dress. The 1559 Injunctions instructed clergy to wear 'seemly habits, garments, and such square caps as were most commonly and orderly received in the latter year of the reign of King Edward'. To some, including the combined fellowship of St John's College, Cambridge, this seemed to smack of Popery. By 1565, the Queen remonstrated with Parker over the lack of conformity. Patently the wearing of a surplice could not be understood as something affecting one's eternal salvation, but it could very easily bring to a head the question of uniformity in the Church.

In Lent 1566, the clergy of London were summoned by Parker and Bishop Grindal (who himself disliked vestments) to observe a correctly attired minister at Lambeth Palace. Thirty-seven clergy were suspended for refusing to wear the canonical garments. This was followed by the Advertisements of 1566 requiring uniformity of practice: 'Every minister saying any public prayers, or ministering the sacraments or any other rites of the Church' was to wear 'a comely surplice with sleeves'. After the crisis many of those who had been removed from office began a preaching campaign. Some looked back to their experience of exile in Mary's reign. One of Grindal's detractors wrote:

> we remembered . . . a congregation at Geneva, which used a book and an order of preaching, ministering of sacraments and discipline, most agreeable to the word of God; which book is allowed by that godly and well-learned man, Master Calvin, and the preachers there; which book and order we now hold. And if you can reprove this book, or anything that we hold, by the word of God, we will yield to you, and do open penance at Paul's Cross; if not, we will stand to it by the grace of God.

The logic was clear: if the Bible did not instruct on something it should not be done – and no civil power had to the right to overrule Scripture in the name of decency and good order.

While none would have denied that the supreme government of the church was to be placed under the authority of Scripture, the logic of the Tudor theory of sovereignty meant that it was up to the Queen, or at least the Queen in Parliament, to determine which doctrines were contained in Scripture. As J. W. Allen wrote many years ago:

Law recognised that the determinations of civil authority concerning religious belief and observance must be consistent with the word of God; and law proceeded to assume that they always were so. The authority of the Scriptures became a kind of legal fiction.

This was at the heart of the Admonitions crisis (1572), which was provoked by a polemic of John Field and Thomas Wilcox. This provides the context for the culmination of the theology of royal absolutism in the theology of Richard Hooker, explored in the next chapter.

Chapter 3
Competing visions for the Church of England

John Whitgift and Thomas Cartwright

If the Queen in Parliament was sovereign over the Church, this gave little room to either clergy or laity (at least those outside Parliament) to exercise much authority. And yet many had experienced something quite different in their sojourns in Europe. There were widespread demands for reform. What was at issue was the question of how much the Church, including its lay members, should be able to decide for itself. The seemingly innocuous Articles XX ('The Church hath power to decree Rites or Ceremonies, and authority in Controversies of Faith') and XXXIV ('It is not necessary that Tradition and Ceremonies be in all places one') had far-reaching consequences for the relationships between Church and state and for the theology of authority.

Thomas Cartwright (1535–1603) was perhaps the most outspoken among the puritan divines. He was deprived of his Cambridge Professorship in 1570, making his way to Geneva and getting to know Calvin's successor, Theodore Beza (1519–1605). For Cartwright, virtually nothing could be regarded as indifferent, including the ministry. The church was understood as a 'democracy' based on the authority of elders elected by the congregation (known as Presbyterianism). The sovereign's role was merely to confirm the action of the church in rooting out sin wherever it was found. To downplay the role of the church in determining law was, he claimed, akin to creating two Gods, a severe God of the law and a gentle God of the Gospel.

Against these charges, Matthew Parker sought out Cartwright's erstwhile Cambridge colleague, the vice-chancellor John Whitgift (1530–1604), to compose a set of replies. The heart of the controversy was over the meaning of the term 'necessary'. The basic point was not that matters 'indifferent' to salvation were not important, but rather they were those things which each and every national church had the authority to alter in due manner. Thus God 'hath not in scripture particularly determined any thing, but left the same to his church, to make or abrogate . . . as shall be thought from time to time most convenient for the present state of the Church'. Order, decency, and discipline were crucial, which meant that even in those things indifferent to salvation, it was still 'the duty of a Christian man without superstition willingly to obey such constitutions'. The freedom of the Gospel did not imply the freedom of the individual.

Whitgift protested against elevating 'indifferent' things into matters of faith. Against those who opposed vestments as unscriptural, he remarked: 'When they were a sign and a token of the popish priesthood, then they were evil . . . but now they be signs and tokens of the ministers of the word of God, which are good, and therefore also they be good'. His opponents could not agree: if the Bible did not expressly teach something then it should simply not be done. The Prayer Book itself, a repository of Reformed doctrine, became a source of controversy because it contained many translations of ancient prayers which could not be found in the Bible. Beza wrote to Archbishop Grindal about the Prayer Book:

> as touching the Lord's supper, who can refrain tears, to declare how miserably it is transformed into that old stagelike frisking and horrible Idol gadding? . . . For who would not think, that the using of an altar, or some table were an indifferent thing? . . . They were

> not content with common and plain songs, and therefore ... that
> busy and curious prickesong and descanting was brought in, more
> meet for stage plays, for the most part, than for an holy action.

The language of the Admonitions was even more direct: the Prayer Book was 'an imperfect book culled and picked out of the popish dunghill the mass book full of abominations'.

Against the puritan insistence on the necessity of Presbyterian church government grounded in Scripture, Whitgift asserted that although government was vital for the good order of the church, its precise form could vary depending on circumstances. According to the Thirty-Nine Articles, the true marks of the church were simply the true preaching of the Word and the right administration of the sacraments, something shared with Luther: 'this or that kind of government' was not of the essence of the church.

> I confess that in a church collected together in one place, and at
> liberty, government is necessary ... but that any kind of
> Government is so necessary that without it the church cannot be
> saved, or that it may not be altered into some other kind thought to
> be more expedient, I utterly deny.

Consequently Whitgift (like Jewel before him) saw no need for uniformity in ministry between different national churches: 'we do not take upon (as we are slandered) either to blame or to condemn other churches, for such orders as they have received most fit for their estates'.

Cartwright answered Whitgift with remarkable speed, defending the Presbyterian system and the equality of ministers as rooted in Scripture. Whitgift's response was clear: it was a matter of prudence for the church to legislate when something was not expressly ruled out by Scripture. Since there was no particular doctrine of ministry in the Bible, it was up to the legitimate authority to ensure that ministry was suited to its context. The most appropriate form was that which was best able to maintain decency and prevent 'subversion and confusion'. Consequently, it was up to the Godly prince to rule the church in matters indifferent through the hierarchy of ministers: 'The prince having the supreme government of the realm, in all causes and over all persons, as she doth exercise the one by the lord chancellor, so doth she the other by the archbishops.' The alternative was for the church to decide for itself – and who could tell what might happen then? As Elizabeth put it: 'They are dangerous to kingly rule, a sect of dangerous consequence, who would have no king but a presbyter.'

The theology of Richard Hooker

Richard Hooker (1553–1600) (Figure 6) continued in a similar vein. The beauty of his language often masks its controversial tone. Hooker was taken under Jewel's wing at Oxford. After ordination he marked himself out as an anti-puritan preacher. In 1586, he became Master of the Temple in London, one of the most important pulpits in the country. He moved to country parishes where he wrote the eight books of his magnum opus, *The Laws of Ecclesiastical Polity*, the last three of which were published posthumously. Hooker's sparring partner was the Cambridge theologian Walter Travers (c. 1548–1635), a friend of Beza. Travers became afternoon lecturer at the Temple. The debates between the two men became famous. It was said by one of Hooker's early biographers: 'the forenoon sermon spake Canterbury; and the afternoon Geneva'. According to Travers, Christ promulgated a perfect law for ruling his Holy Commonwealth, which was to be exercised by elders, who had their authority conferred on them not by the king but by the people. The state had duties to protect the church but not to control it. Hooker wrote his *Ecclesiastical Polity* to counter such contentions: each of the last seven books is given a heading that summarizes some part of the puritan position followed by Hooker's attempts to destroy it. Book I amounts to a philosophy of law and the use of reason in solving disputes. Where Travers regarded 'supernaturally revealed' law as the most important and

6. Richard Hooker was the greatest theological defender of the Church of England as a national church

fundamental, Hooker was able to show how God had given to his creatures the capacity to establish laws for regulating their affairs which were not based directly on revelation, but on reason. While some forms of law are necessary for human survival, there are others which reason teaches to be 'fit and convenient'. An example is the law of inheritance: each society needs a clear system of inheritance in which no rational law is transgressed, although these laws vary from commonwealth to commonwealth. Without this there would be anarchy. The final sections of Book I develop this method in relation to the delineation of what is necessary to salvation and other forms of necessity which have to be established on the basis of reason. Reason fills in the particulars where Scripture is silent. Hooker also tries to show that reason is required to legislate not merely in that huge range of matters where Scripture is silent, but also to work out the 'drift' of Scripture in the first place.

In the remaining seven books, Hooker sets about relating this theory to the contested issues. Book III, for instance, discusses church order, differentiating between things necessary to salvation and 'accessory' matters: matters of church order depend on human reason rather than divine injunction. In the next two books, Hooker defends the right of the national church to decide for itself in such matters:

> The church hath authority to establish that for an order at one time which at another time it may abolish, and in both may do well . . . Laws touching matter of order are changeable, by the power of the church; articles concerning doctrine not so.

Nevertheless, the church should be loath to change its principles 'unless some notable public inconvenience enforce the contrary'. He discusses a wide range of issues, particularly the sacraments, where he makes much of the notion of mutual participation which gives believers a real 'infused' power to live the new life. In the eucharist he develops a notion of the real presence dependent on the Holy Spirit, the power of Christ, and the faith of the receiver: while undoubtedly reformed in his sympathies, Hooker displays a strong conservatism, holding back from the more radical theories of his own time.

Books VI and VII discuss the problem of ministry. While bishops are useful and have been in existence for a long time, it is nevertheless possible to change the ministry if circumstances should require. For the time being, however, episcopacy is the best way of keeping order, providing a 'sufficient remedy' for the 'emulations, strifes and contentious authority' of alternative forms of church government. In the final book, Hooker defends the right of the prince to legislate for the church, attacking the separation of the realms of church and state:

> There is not any man of the Church of England but the same man is also a member of the commonwealth; nor any man a member of the commonwealth which is not also of the Church of England.

Bishops do not hold their authority directly from Christ, but are granted it from the spiritual community which is based on the general consent of all people. This leads Hooker to a defence of the Royal Supremacy over the church. The king, the 'common parent', has the lawful power 'to order and dispose of spiritual affairs'. Authority in both church and state thus derives from one source: the sovereign in parliament.

In some ways Hooker is the convergence point of many competing and not necessarily reconcilable ideas: in him one can find the stoic-natural law tradition; the Augustinian emphasis on the need for government as a remedy for human sin; the harmony of natural and supernatural ends (which is similar to that of Thomas Aquinas); the Roman lawyer's belief in untrammelled sovereignty; but also the feudal lawyer's belief in contract and consent. What unites it all is that there is simply no room for disorder or for alternative ways of understanding the world. Uniformity under the monarch is everything: this is perhaps the furthest extension of Troeltsch's idea of the church. How much longer such an idea could survive, however, was an open question. After all, many had quite different pictures of what the Church of England should look like.

James I

After Elizabeth died in 1603, the Crown passed to the Stuart Kings of Scotland. It might have been expected that James would be keen on reforming the English Church along the Scottish model. However, he had spent a significant period trying to reinvigorate the Scottish episcopate and to counter the claims of the Kirk over the Scottish monarchy. He strongly upheld the Divine Right of Kings: 'Kings are called Gods by the prophetical King David, because they sit upon God his throne in the earth.' Shortly after James's accession, an effort was made at Hampton Court to reconcile the different ecclesiastical factions. The leading puritan spokesman was John Reynolds (President of Corpus Christi College, Oxford) who insisted on purity of doctrine and an able clergy accountable to laity, as well as the correction of what he regarded as the errors of the Prayer Book. The leading episcopal spokesmen were Lancelot Andrewes, Bishop of Winchester, and Richard Bancroft (1544–1610), who succeeded Whitgift in 1604. In the end the puritans agreed to obey the King, who, while making virtually no concessions, allowed for the toleration of tender consciences for a while. The Conference also set up a committee of scholars of different theological persuasions to produce an authoritative translation of the English Bible (the Authorized Version of 1611). The puritans achieved very little and, instead of looking to the King, many turned instead to the Parliament.

Bancroft set about codifying canon law, reaffirming the Crown's 'ancient jurisdiction over the state ecclesiastical'. The new canons included many of the injunctions and advertisements from previous reigns, but also sought to improve the exercise of ministry, for example by ending non-residence for the clergy. They were, however, uncompromising on vestments and holy tables, which were to be placed in the chancel. No longer was the church simply that place where the Word was purely preached and the sacrament duly celebrated, but rather it was visibly structured according to certain ceremonies and rites and patrolled by bishops. The demand for the increase in clerical income was not met: Parliament, many of whose members had benefited greatly from the redistribution of ecclesiastical revenues, refused to redirect money back to the Church. Without the consent of Parliament, Bancroft had to use the old systems to improve the clerical lot, and rejuvenated the episcopal visitation system to ensure conformity. Parliament also declined to increase the coercive power of the ecclesiastical courts against the power of the civil courts: a stronger Church would mean a weaker Parliament. The battle lines were being drawn.

Doctrinal controversy

George Abbot (1562–1633) succeeded Bancroft in 1611. His time as Archbishop was characterized by disputes over the doctrine of election and predestination. After 1611, when European alliances were of decisive importance, a major pan-Protestant dispute emerged across northern Europe which divided many in the English Church. The conflict centred on the teachings of the Dutch theologian Jacobus Arminius (1560–1609). Against the Calvinists, Arminians believed that even the elect could fall from grace, and that the non-elect were damned because of their own sins rather than from all eternity. This allowed for a certain degree of free will: God's grace could be resisted. Christ died for all, even though none but the faithful could enjoy the pardon of sin.

The Synod of Dort (1618–19) was convened to resolve these doctrinal questions. Bishop George Carleton of Llandaff, who represented the English Church, pursued the rigidly Calvinist line which was ratified by the Synod. Faith was understood as a gift of God that was given to some but not to others. This election was made before the foundation of the world: the elect were determined to everlasting life, and the non-elect to everlasting death. Christ's atonement was for the elect alone. Those whom God had chosen nevertheless had to persevere in their faith, a gift bestowed by God. Even though there was no official ratification of the Synod in England, it nevertheless shaped theology profoundly in the years to come, so much so that most clergy in the period probably accepted this so-called double predestination.

The effects of the doctrine on the Church of England were not clear-cut. It was, after all, difficult to reconcile the church of the elect with obedience to a national church made up of saints and sinners alike. In distinction, the Arminian notion, which accepted a universality of salvation and the possibility of co-operation with God's grace, placed great stress on the obedience to the divinely appointed authority. The controversialist lawyer John Selden noted the irony of this position:

> The puritans who will allow no free-will at all, but God does all, yet will allow the subject his liberty to do or not to do, notwithstanding the king, the god upon earth. The Arminians, who hold we have free-will, yet say, when we come to the king there must be all obedience, and no liberty must be stood for.

The church of all true believers, which for the Calvinists was located in an invisible realm known alone to God, became in Arminianism the *visible* church in which all endeavoured to live freely in accordance with the divine will.

It was not long before there were moves away from rigid Calvinism. This expressed itself in what has been called 'avant-garde conformism'. Many sought to re-order church buildings. Richard Neile, Bishop of Durham (1617–28), for instance, moved the communion table into an 'altarwise' position up against the east end of the church rather than 'tablewise' in the chancel (Figure 7), and in 1620 rebuilt a stone altar.

This emphasized the importance of the sacraments as a means of grace. In the 1620s, anti-Calvinists were promoted, including William Laud (1573–1645), who became bishop of St David's, and Richard Montagu, who became Bishop of Chichester in 1627. Charles I, who succeeded to the throne in 1625, had Abbot

7. **Chancel of Hailes Church, Gloucestershire. The communion table is set 'tablewise' in the chancel, as suggested in the second Book of Common Prayer.**

suspended (for accidentally killing a gamekeeper) and the archepiscopate was exercised by a commission.

The later years of James's reign and the early years of Charles's saw a flowering of theology and spirituality, particularly among a small group of well-educated churchmen, often known as the Caroline Divines. For men like Jeremy Taylor and Lancelot Andrewes, the emphasis was on regular prayer, a high view of the sacraments and episcopate, knowledge of the Fathers, and the 'practice of the presence of God'. Some later thinkers, particularly from Anglo-Catholic backgrounds, have seen them as embodying the heart of Anglican spirituality, although they typify a very one-sided way of understanding the reformed theology of the Prayer Book.

One of their number, William Laud, was elevated to London in 1629 and then to Canterbury in 1633. His opinions were clear. As early as 1626, he defended royal power and obedience: the church and state 'are so nearly united and knit together' that 'the Church

Cathedrals

A distinctive feature of the Church of England, compared with almost all other reformed churches, has been the survival of cathedrals. Some, including Diarmaid MacCulloch, have seen them as the 'cuckoos in the nest' of Protestantism. Although statutes were reformed in 1540 and the old monastic houses dissolved, large sums of money were still channelled to deans and canons. Henry VIII established six new cathedrals with his monastic spoils (although Westminster Abbey survived as a cathedral for a mere ten years). Cathedral clergy served outside the parish system, and often functioned as a liturgical and theological avant-garde. A high standard of choral music persisted in cathedrals and the other non-parochial churches, such as the Chapels Royal or Westminster Abbey, perhaps because of Elizabeth I's love of music.

As is satirized in Anthony Trollope's Barchester novels, large endowments continued through to the 19th century, when finally the number of canons was restricted to no more than six and large sums were redistributed to the wider church to endow poorer parishes. Even into the 20th century, many of the most influential church leaders have served as deans (like Hewlett Johnson, the 'red dean' of Canterbury) or canons of cathedrals (like John Collins, the peace activist and canon of St Paul's). Cathedrals remain great patrons of the arts to the present day.

[may] call in the help of the State', and the state may call in the service of the church, 'both to teach that duty which her Members know not, and to exhort them to, and to encourage them in that duty they know'. In London, Laud made a number of changes: ministers were to be called priests, 'saint' was to be abbreviated not by the English 'St' but by the Latin (and thus Roman-sounding) 'S.'. The St Gregory's case in London forced communion tables to be set 'altarwise' at the east end of the church, emphasizing 'the external decent worship of God'. Several bishops encouraged the building of altars, most importantly Matthew Wren at Norwich and William Peirce at Bath and Wells. Recent scholars have suggested that these policies of clerical aggrandizement and imposition of conformity were important causes of the Civil War. There was a very rapid destabilization of the fragile ecclesiastical peace of the earlier years of the 17th century.

Laud's theology continued in the same polemical vein as Jewel and Hooker. His major theological work, the *Conference with Mr Fisher the Jesuit*, is an apology for the independent authority of each national church. All churches are equal: indeed, there is no universal church apart from its existence in particular churches. While the church might be preserved in its totality from error, this did not mean that any one part, or even a general council, was guaranteed of truth, as Article XXI had asserted. It was crucial that, where the universal church refuses to reform itself, the particular must set about this task. While Laud may have been a theorist of the autonomy of each church (even if he tried to make Scotland and Ireland dependent on Canterbury), he also had a high view of his own role and that of his royal master in the process of reform.

The breakdown of the royal system

To some, the imposition of conformity was little short of Catholicism in disguise. In the 1630s ecclesiastical policy led to the persecution of puritans and the silencing of other voices, including the Calvinism of Bishop Davenant of Salisbury. In 1633, the Book of

Sports was re-issued which permitted lawful recreation on Sundays, challenging the sabbatarianism of the puritans. The situation worsened with the imposition of the Scottish Book of Common Prayer which bypassed the General Assembly. The new Canons of 1640 made matters even worse, reasserting the Divine Right of the King and attempting to ensure uniformity. Laud's system was simple: 'First [came] the magistrate, and his power and justice. And resist either of these, and ye resist the power, and the ordinance of God.' Many English people, however, were no longer prepared to accept such obedience.

After the outbreak of war, there were efforts to reform the Church of England. This led to the Westminster Assembly, a Synod of 30 lay assessors and over 120 divines of different opinions, which met over 1,000 times until 1653. The attempt to reform the Thirty-Nine Articles along solidly Reformed lines produced the Westminster Confession in 1646. This emphasized the invisible church against the visible church of the Laudian period. Richard Baxter, one of the leading puritans, praised the Assembly: 'the Christian world since the days of the apostles had never had a synod of more excellent divines (taking one thing with another) than this synod and the synod of Dort'. The Book of Common Prayer was banned in 1645 and in its place the Assembly produced a *Directory for the Public Worship of God*, which contained more general instructions than forms of service. The *Directory* proved remarkably ineffectual: in many places the Prayer Book continued to be used in private. Some saw the Westminster Assembly simply as the replacement of the old priest with the new presbyter. Its attempts at comprehensiveness, according to Milton, were characterized by 'plots and packings worse than Trent'. Many later attempts at conciliation collapsed: there were far more extreme measures against the King and the Church, most importantly the execution of William Laud and eventually of the King.

Oliver Cromwell himself did not push ecclesiastical reform as far as he might. While many sought to deprive all clergy and to abandon parishes, Cromwell retained a territorial system and ensured that tithes continued to be collected. Although all churches were theoretically independent, there was nevertheless the continuation of the rights of advowson (of appointing clergy by a patron), with Cromwell exercising Crown appointments. A national church was preserved, although doctrinally it was relatively diffuse. To ensure that there was some degree of consistency, a National Committee of Triers and local Committees of Ejectors were established. Some 2,000 to 3,000 'malignant' and 'scandalous' clergy were expelled and new clergy put in their place. Evidence of God's grace became the chief criterion for ministry: 'they must not admit a man unless they be able to discern some of the grace of God in him'. After the end of the Protectorate, selection of ministers was less rigorous.

What became obvious during the period of the Civil War and Cromwell's rule was that things would never be quite the same again: the number of independently minded ministers and their relative success during this period meant that ultimately some degree of tolerance could not be denied to them. As the historian Norman Sykes wrote:

> For better and for worse the Tudor theory of the identity of Church and State had been finally shattered; and the future pattern of English religious life was never to approach the ideal of *ein Reich, ein Volk, eine Kirche*.

The Restoration settlement and the end of the national church

After Cromwell's death in 1658, it became obvious that the days of the interregnum were numbered. Given that there was a Presbyterian majority in Parliament, and that Parliament would have to agree before there could be any return to monarchy, some form of Presbyterian polity which was relatively tolerant of other views might have been expected. Had Parliament insisted on this, it is difficult to see how Charles II could have refused. Charles initially intended to return with an act of indulgence towards those who dissented from the Church of England to 'gratify the private consciences of those who are aggrieved with the use of some ceremonies'. There was to be a diversity over the old bugbears, including the wearing of the surplice, the sign of the cross at baptism, bowing at the holy name, and kneeling at communion. All that mattered was that there should be an agreement on fundamentals. Bishoprics were offered to the leading Presbyterians, Richard Baxter (who declined) and Edward Reynolds, who became Bishop of Norwich.

To discuss the matter of religion, a conference was held at the Savoy in London in 1661. Twelve theologians attended from each side. The Presbyterians set about producing objections to the Prayer Book which led to the 'Savoy Book', which was more Genevan in tone than the Tudor Prayer Books. They also made other demands, including freedom from oaths and acceptance of non-episcopal ordinations. In the end, particularly under the influence of John Cosin, who challenged Baxter to state exactly where the Prayer Book contravened the Word of God, there was little agreement on the contentious points:

> We were all agreed on the ends, for the Church's welfare, Unity and
> Peace, and His Majesty's Happiness and Contentment, but after all
> our debates, were disagreed of the means. And this was the end of
> that Assembly and Commission.

Sheldon, Bishop of London, dominated the proceedings and Baxter was persuaded to adjourn the Conference, which proved a fatal mistake.

The so-called Cavalier Parliament went far further than the King ever intended. Supporters of the old church order dominated Parliament, particularly after the return of the bishops. Attempts at reconciliation proved fruitless and a stern Act of Uniformity was passed in 1662. All ministers had to be ordained by bishops, and all clergy had to take an oath of 'unfeigned assent and consent to all and everything contained and prescribed in' the Prayer Book. The new book added a service of baptism for those of riper years (to bring back anabaptists into the Church of England) and also a revised Black Rubric in which the words 'real and essential' were changed to 'corporal', thereby allowing belief in a very moderate form of real presence.

Over the period some 1,760 incumbents were deprived of their livings. While the number who finally became nonconformists is difficult to gauge, it nevertheless reveals the fiction of a national church: there were simply too many dissenters to be contained. The idea of the Restoration Church as a monolithic church is distant from the actual situation. Its initial triumph seems to have been based more on fear than anything else, although there were efforts to encourage devotion to the royal cult of Charles the Martyr, formally canonized by Parliament as 'saint and martyr'. As John Spurr put it:

> The settlement of 1662 was a political, indeed an Erastian, solution to the religious divisions of the English; moreover, it was based on a conspicuously narrower interest than was the political settlement. None of this augured well for its stability or survival.

After this time various Acts of Parliament (the so-called Clarendon Code) tried to suppress dissent altogether. In 1661, the Corporation Act required all people taking municipal office to receive holy communion. The Five Mile Act ensured that nonconformist ministers and schoolmasters lived outside corporate towns. The Conventicle Act of 1670 sought to abolish 'seditious sectaries', imposing fines for public worship of more than five people.

Cranmer's dilemma returns?

Things grew more incoherent in the late 1680s when Charles II's successor, James II, openly practised as a Roman Catholic. This raised questions about the role of the King as Supreme Governor of the Church of England. Cranmer's dilemma returned: so much energy had been invested in the Stuart family and in their divine right to rule, that when it was fatally compromised there was little choice but to support the *coup d'état* of 1688 which brought William and Mary to the throne.

8. St Mary's Church, Ingestre, Staffordshire, by Christopher Wren. To receive communion one has to pass under the royal coat of arms – the national church has become the established church.

The Toleration Act that followed in 1689 exempted 'their majesties' Protestant subjects dissenting from the Church of England from the penalties of certain laws', provided that they took the oaths of allegiance and supremacy. Freedom to worship was allowed for Trinitarian groups (but not to non-Trinitarians or Roman Catholics). Ministers had to subscribe to all but four of the Thirty-Nine Articles (or five for Baptists). What was enacted, according to Spurr, was the product of a Parliament that 'understood Anglicanism as a badge of political and ideological trustworthiness; widening the terms of communion meant widening access to office; but a toleration would simply allow freedom of worship, while restricting political power to safe hands. The cost to the church of England was incalculable.'

What had effectively happened was that the national church had become the established church (Figure 8): this amounted to a legal recognition of the situation which had existed at least since the early 1640s. While there were many in England who were not members of the Church of England, the exercise of all forms of political power was still dependent on receiving the Anglican sacraments: the Test Act of 1673 (where all officeholders had to take the sacrament) and the Corporation Act were not abolished until 1828. At the same time the possibility of comprehension had disappeared. The implications of the 1688–9 revolution were massive, shaping the Church of England into one denomination among others, albeit one with many privileges.

Chapter 4
Evangelicalism

Church parties

It is hardly surprising that a church claiming some sort of identity with a nation should always have been composed of people of markedly different opinions. Before 1689, however, nearly everybody shared a vision of the unity of all Christians in England (even when those visions differed). Many commentators have noted that the Act of Toleration brought with it a fundamental change. The political historian J. N. Figgis, for instance, saw a profound change in the nature of ecclesiastical sovereignty in the 18th century: even though each denomination might claim an exclusive possession of the truth, the fact of plurality forced a degree of toleration. Religion was ultimately a matter of choice. It was the Toleration Act and 'not any bigotry of high and low, which has made the church a small society, relatively . . . The Church of England may still be established, but it is only one society among others.' All the church could hope for was that it would become one group among many, since it was no longer possible to impose the will of one particular society on the whole. Wherever there was liberty of conscience the church inevitably became a voluntary organization and more sectarian. Although 'people dislike calling [the contemporary church] a sect or a denomination, it can be nothing else, so long as there are large numbers who repudiate all part or lot in it and in many cases detest its ideals'. For Figgis, this process would lead to the decay of conventional religion and the advent of smaller, but more serious alternatives. This use of the term 'sect' was in no way pejorative, and displays a strong similarity to the definition given by Ernst Troeltsch of sects as

> comparatively small groups; they aspire after personal inward perfection, and they aim at a direct personal fellowship between the members of each group. From the very beginning they are forced to organize themselves in small groups, and to renounce the idea of dominating the world.

From the 18th century onwards, there was a struggle for identity in the Church of England. This was combined with frequent questioning of the national church ideal by those who sought a 'real' rather than a nominal form of Christianity. It is in this context that one can begin to understand church parties. While church parties have family resemblances to the groups that went before, there are also fundamental differences. What characterized the modern church party was its clamour for an authority and an identity that was distinct from the wider church and nation, and where partisan identity was sometimes as important, or even more important, than ecclesiastical identity. A longing for identity led to the proliferation of party organizations and groups and a form of voluntarism quite distinct from the compulsory church of earlier years. The religion of the Church of England gradually came to be seen by many as a distinctive form of life which required a commitment greater than that required simply to be English. What began as a revival transformed itself into a group with strict membership criteria which sought to oppose the alternatives. Indeed, parties sometimes almost became churches within churches. This is as true for Evangelicals, who will be discussed in this chapter, as it is for Anglo-Catholics, who form the subject of the next.

Problems during the 18th century

The Church of England's identity was defined in the years before 1689 through its relationship with the different power interests of the church and state. In the 18th century, however, things gradually began to change. On the one hand, a not insignificant number, including about three to four hundred clergy, refused to acknowledge the rights of the new King and Queen and formed the group of 'non-jurors'. Others sought a new settlement that would give the church and monarch a certain degree of independence from the government: this group (the High Churchmen) was almost synonymous with the Tories, who fought against the encroachments of the Whig government. Some others (the Low Churchmen) proved far more inclined to accept a stronger Parliament ruling directly over the church, especially after the proroguing of Convocation in 1717. It would be quite wrong to suppose that the Hanoverian church was moribund and simply a political tool: there were many earnest and devoted churchmen working within the established church. Many took the sacraments and theology seriously, and many worked tirelessly throughout the country, often suffering financial hardship in poorly endowed parishes. Some, including Archbishop Wake, began ecumenical discussions with overseas churches.

However, others sought a form of Christian identity different from that of the past. Both inside and outside the established church, Evangelicalism, the first of the great religious revivals, was marked by a form of religious authority based on the security of a personal religious experience as a marker of authenticity. Bishop J. C. Ryle wrote in 1898 that a 'leading feature of Evangelical religion is the high place which is assigned to the Holy Spirit in the heart of man . . . there can be no real conversion to God, no new creation in Christ, no new birth of the spirit, where there is nothing felt within.' Not surprisingly, Evangelicalism became a religion of the powerful hearts of big personalities. That, coupled with a new sense of seriousness, meant that many Evangelicals soon set about reforming the church and the world. Where earlier Church of England controversies had focused primarily on church order and authority, Evangelicals stressed lifestyle, doctrine, and conduct.

From the mid-18th century a number of clergy began to introduce reforms into their parishes. William Grimshaw, incumbent of Haworth in Yorkshire from 1742 until his death in 1763, took his charge seriously, increasing the numbers of communicants from twelve on his arrival to well over a thousand. Like many other Evangelicals, he was an activist. In the words of an obituarist, he was 'one of the most laborious and indefatigable ministers I have ever known'. Henry Venn (1729–1797) was equally active in Huddersfield from 1759 to 1771, after a period at Clapham. For some Evangelicals there was a sense of optimism: the Christian duty was to co-operate with God's grace through the salvation wrought in Christ, which meant that Christians could live the life of holiness. And holiness would lead, as John Wesley put it, to happiness. It was for this reason, as Venn remarked, that the children of God know more of true happiness than anybody else. Writings thus tended to be practical, as with Venn's influential *Complete Duty of Man*, a popular guide to Christian living: there were far fewer of the great feats of learning undertaken by the clergy of previous generations. Both Grimshaw and Venn subscribed to independent chapels to ensure that a proper Evangelical tradition of preaching would continue after their incumbency. They were also both itinerant preachers.

Henry Venn's son, John (1759–1813), became Rector of Holy Trinity Church, Clapham, in 1792, where a number of prominent professionals formed a circle that was nicknamed the Clapham Sect. Most important of these was William Wilberforce, MP for Hull and author in 1797 of *A Practical View of the Prevailing Religious Systems in Higher and Middle Classes in this Country contrasted with Real Christianity*. This distinction between nominal and real Christianity was a central feature of Evangelical religion, and ushered in a recognition that all was not well with the world. A sense of moral earnestness led to campaigns in Parliament and elsewhere. Vast sums were given to charities, including missions and schools. Most important of all was the campaign to abolish the trade in slaves which Wilberforce carried through the House of Commons in 1807. For Wilberforce, writing in his *Letter on the Abolition of the Slave Trade*, Christ has 'made all mankind one great family, all our fellow creatures are now our brethren'. By 1833, slavery was finally abolished in the British Empire. Other activities included the first factory legislation as well as societies founded to help the destitute and the poor.

Wilberforce's friend, Hannah More, was another great activist for whom 'Action is the life of virtue and the world is the theatre of action'. She worked tirelessly in Somerset for the education of the poor as well as producing the Cheap Repository Tracts which used stories to make moral points. John Venn similarly established parochial schools: education was conceived as a preparation for the Gospel. Among the early Evangelicals there was a highly moralistic programme that was organized into a Society for the Suppression of Vice which campaigned against indecency and profanation of the Lord's Day. Alongside this was an emphasis on prayers in the family, and domestic religion. Henry Thornton, another member of the Clapham Sect, produced the best-selling *Family Prayers*. Self-examination and diary-keeping proved popular pastimes. A moral earnestness was exhibited, sometimes in unusual ways. It is said that James Stephen, a prominent member of the Sect, once smoked a cigar, but finding it so enjoyable, never smoked another.

While there was undoubtedly a paternalistic flavour to much of the activity of the Clapham Sect and little acceptance of democracy, there was nevertheless a genuine humanitarianism that could treat all people as brothers and sisters under God. The radical William Cobbett's accusation that the mission of the 'Saints' (as the Clapham Sect was also known) 'was to teach people to starve without making a noise and keeping the poor from cutting the throats of the rich' is unfair. The example of the Clapham Sect was followed by the undoubted lay leader of the next generation, Anthony Ashley Cooper (1801–85), later Earl of Shaftesbury, one of an increasing number of Evangelical MPs. He worked persistently for the improvement of conditions in factories and among labourers.

Insiders and outsiders

If activism was one strand characterizing early Evangelicalism, another, probably more far-reaching, emphasis was that of deciding who was inside and who was outside the church. This is the most obvious example of sectarianism in Evangelicalism. From the beginning, Evangelicals agreed on the importance of conversion: there was a point at which the individual came to accept his or her own salvation. John Wesley's conversion is probably the best known:

> I felt my heart strangely warmed. I felt I did trust in Christ, Christ alone for salvation: And an assurance was given me, that he had taken away my sins, even mine, and saved me from the law of sin and death.

Wesley had been a devout priest for some ten years, but what had changed was a personal awareness of sins forgiven. It was such an assurance that marked out real from nominal Christianity: 'By a Christian,' he wrote, 'I mean one who so believes in Christ that sin had no more dominion over him: and in this sense of the word I was not a Christian till May 24th [1738].' Conversion soon became the test of Evangelical belonging; testifying and witnessing to a change of heart, and allowing this change of heart to control one's whole life, dominated Evangelical piety; the chief object of preaching was to win over converts. One of the leading Evangelicals of the 19th century, Robert Bickersteth, Bishop of Ripon from 1857 to 1884, held that 'no sermon was worthy of the name which did not contain the message of the Gospel, urging the sinner to be reconciled with God'.

Where infant baptism had been traditionally understood as the mark of entry into the church, this extra requirement led to a considerable amount of controversy. The problem was clearly stated by Henry Ryder, the first Evangelical bishop, who complained against the 'most serious error of contemplating all the individuals of a baptised congregation, as converted'. Things came to a head in the Gorham Judgement. In 1847, George Cornelius Gorham was presented to the living of Brampford Speke in Devon. Henry Phillpotts, Bishop of Exeter, insisted on examining him before his induction as vicar. Gorham, it turned out, held that infants never benefited from baptism unless there was some other gift of grace. Phillpotts refused to induct him on the grounds that this contradicted the Prayer Book doctrine of baptismal regeneration.

Gorham took the case to the Court of Arches, where the bishop's case was upheld. This was overturned in 1850 by the Privy Council: 'the grace of regeneration does not so necessarily accompany the act of baptism that regeneration invariably takes place in baptism . . . in no case is regeneration unconditional'. Eventually, Gorham was instituted by Archbishop Sumner, an Evangelical. During the case the Archbishop's brother, Charles, Bishop of Winchester, wrote of the need for conversion: 'I must look, notwithstanding his baptism, for the Scriptural evidence of his being a child of God.' For some, the encroachment of secular courts on doctrine was the last straw. This 'vile judgement' led to Henry Manning's departure for Rome. The case was also an important factor in reviving Convocation as the church's independent voice.

Similar views have been maintained by many Evangelicals since. In recent years, Bishop Colin Buchanan has been a great campaigner for tightening up the boundaries of the church. In speaking of moral breakdown and the rising number of unmarried parents, Buchanan wrote 'it is at least arguable that nothing will solve such a situation except a true conversion to Christ; and a connivance by the Church, without conversion in one or both parents, will deceive them, their child, and anyone else asking for baptism also'. The world will be saved only by conversion to Christ and baptism is predicated on this conversion.

Charles Simeon

The most influential leader of Anglican Evangelicalism was Charles Simeon (1759–1836) (Figure 9), Fellow of King's College, Cambridge, and Perpetual Curate at Holy Trinity Church from 1782 to 1836. His description of his conversion in 1779 as an undergraduate reveals something of the early evangelical soul: 'The thought came to my mind, "What, may I transfer all my guilt to another? Has God provided an offering for me, that I may lay my sins on his head?" Then, God willing, I will not bear them on my own soul one moment longer.' Personal conviction led to a life of action. Simeon's preaching shaped a couple of generations of Cambridge undergraduates, and his ability to channel funds to the Evangelical cause affected even the remotest part of the country. The Simeon Trust, formed with money left by his brother, was the first of the ecclesiastical party trusts: by the time of his death, there were 42 livings under its control, including important churches like Bath Abbey, Cheltenham, and Derby.

Together with several members of the Clapham Sect, Simeon was also instrumental in establishing the Church Missionary Society in 1799, which meant that there was some withdrawal of support from the interdenominational London Missionary Society. The new Society, which was founded 'on the Church Principle' rather than the 'High Church Principle' of the existing Society for the Propagation of the Gospel in Foreign Parts (see Chapter 6), provided many of the personnel for the new missions in India, Africa, and Australia. Members of the Clapham Sect, especially Charles Grant, who became a Director of the East India Company, were influential in ensuring that chaplains accompanied the traders. They also established Sierra Leone as a home for ex-slaves,

I. KAY. 1798.

9. Charles Simeon was the formative influence behind Anglican Evangelicalism

and over 18,000 had been settled there by 1825. Members of the Clapham Sect were also responsible for founding the British and Foreign Bible Society which rapidly set about providing Bibles in different languages for the newly planted churches.

Many Evangelicals in the first years of the 19th century began to interpret Scripture in terms of its supposed predictions of the end-times. A revolutionary age led many to read their own times using the Book of Revelation as a guide. While some formed new sects (including the Church of Ireland priest J. N. Darby, who founded the Plymouth Brethren), others sought to influence the Church of England. In 1809, a number of Evangelicals set up the London Society for the Promotion of Christianity Amongst the Jews. Preaching campaigns were held across the country, many, including Simeon, adopting a theology based on the restoration of the Jews to Palestine, making use of a particular reading of the Book of Revelation. A leading Evangelical, Edward Bickersteth, published *The Restoration of the Jews to Their Own Land and the Final Blessedness of the Earth* in 1841. In the late 1830s, Shaftesbury encouraged Lord Palmerston, Foreign Secretary, to sponsor Jewish settlement. Restorationist theology also provided one of the reasons behind the Anglo-Prussian bishopric of Jerusalem, and the building of Christ Church, Jerusalem, where it has continued. The first bishop, appointed in 1841, was the ex-rabbi Michael Solomon Alexander, a Prussian subject living in England.

Like many of the puritans before them, Evangelicals sought to revitalize the authority of Scripture. Although Henry Venn referred to the Bible as the 'infallible word of God', it would be wrong to see the early Evangelicals adopting what would later be called fundamentalism. Both Simeon and Daniel Wilson, Vicar of Islington and later Bishop of Calcutta, acknowledged the importance of human agency in the transmission and interpretation of Scripture. Literal inerrancy came later in the 19th century, particularly under the more hard-line group who supported the newspaper *The Record* and who gradually became the dominant force in Evangelicalism. An example is Joseph Baylee, first Principal of St Aidan's Theological College (for non-graduates), Birkenhead, who claimed to his students that the Bible 'can have no mistake in history, no error in science, no corruption in morals, no deficiency in metaphysics, no ignorance respecting heaven'. Anxious about alternative sources of authority, Ryle suggested that:

Infallibility is not to be found in ordained men, but in the Bible . . . Let no man disturb our souls by such vague expressions as 'the Voice of the Church', primitive antiquity, the judgement of the early Fathers, and the like tall talk. Let our only standard of truth be the Bible, God's Word written.

Evangelical power

It took a number of years for Evangelicalism to make itself felt on the episcopal bench in England: Henry Ryder was appointed in 1815 to Gloucester after some prevarication by the Prime Minister, Lord Liverpool, on the grounds that he was a 'religious bishop'. He held undoubted Evangelical views, including the need for a conversion separate from baptism. It was more than ten years before another Evangelical was appointed in the person of Charles Sumner, to Llandaff in 1826. He moved to the huge diocese of Winchester the following year. His wife, Mary, founded the Mothers' Union, one of the first church organizations established specifically for women. His brother, John, was appointed in 1828 to Chester and in 1848 translated to Canterbury. A vigorous opponent of ritualism, he was Archbishop during the time of the Gorham affair. Other Evangelical bishops quickly followed, especially during the Prime Ministership of Lord Palmerston, whose knowledge of the church was so slim that he relied on his step son-in-law, Lord Shaftesbury, for nominations: from 1856 to 1860, no fewer than six evangelicals were appointed as bishops.

These Evangelical Bishops were frequently hostile to anything that seemed to downplay the Protestant inheritance of the Church of England. As Charles Sumner put it in 1845, the first duty of clergy was to 'vindicate the anti-Roman character of our own church, and next, to guard against the excessive pretensions of such a power as Romanism'. As late as 1867, Samuel Waldegrave, Bishop of Carlisle, could see the wearing of a surplice in the pulpit as 'inseparably associated with the tendencies to the Romish error and superstition'. A later bishop, Edward Henry Bickersteth, wrote that

'A very large number of us believe the Church of Rome to be the Babylon of the Apocalypse . . . We are Protestants, and we are not afraid of the name.' What marked out Evangelicalism was the belief in the Bible, justification by faith, episcopal government, 'and protest with our Articles and homilies against the church of Rome'.

Some towns became virtual Evangelical fiefdoms, including the new town of Cheltenham, which was dominated by Francis Close (1797–1882), incumbent from 1826 for 30 years when he became Dean of Carlisle. He built four new churches as well as a number of schools. He spoke out vehemently against ritualism, giving a sermon on Guy Fawkes Day 1844, entitled 'The Restoration of Churches is the Restoration of Popery'. He railed against those who wore 'meretricious decorations' or transformed the 'Church's servants into Popish or Jewish, sacrificing and interceding priests'. For Close, all answers were to be found in the Bible, since all 'Scripture is given by inspiration of God'. The whole Bible had only one author – the Holy Spirit.

By the end of the 19th century, the leader of the Evangelicals was J. C. Ryle, Disraeli's nomination as first Bishop of Liverpool. A great writer of tracts and popular works, he remained an implacable opponent of anything that smacked of ritualism. As bishop, he took a strong stand against the real presence in the eucharist, a typical Evangelical emphasis which had provoked considerable controversy during the Denison case in the 1850s. He helped to found Evangelical theological colleges, including Wycliffe Hall at Oxford and Ridley Hall in Cambridge, to counter the effects of the diocesan colleges, most of which had fallen into the hands of the ritualists.

Modern Evangelicalism

By the end of the 19th century, Evangelicalism had been transformed into a movement which was defined in terms of its opposition to ritualism, but also as something which focused on rallies of the like-minded. Conferences were held at Mildmay and later in Oxford and Brighton. Anglicans also played an important part in the Keswick Conventions, influenced by the pan-Evangelical holiness movement. Such rallies helped provide an identity for an Evangelicalism that felt beleaguered by the growing success of ritualism.

In the 20th century, some of those things that had provoked the most bitter hostility from Evangelicals had been accepted as commonplaces by other members of the Church of England. As ritualist practices spread far beyond the exotic churches of avant-garde Anglo-Catholicism, it was hardly surprising that a fortress-like mentality took hold among Evangelicals. Fewer and fewer of their leaders were prepared to make the necessary compromises required to enter into the hierarchy. Many sought for greater purity against contamination from those of other opinions. Henry Wace (1836–1924), Dean of Canterbury, for instance, led opposition in Convocation to Modernists like Hensley Henson, calling for repeated subscription to the Creeds.

While some, including the Group Brotherhood, were prepared to adopt a more critical study of the Bible (coalescing around a collection of essays, *Liberal Evangelicalism*, of 1923), most viewed a move away from strict penal substitutionary atonement (where Christ accepted the punishment due to his fellow humans, another characteristic of Evangelical theology) and infallibility of Scripture as the very beginnings of unbelief altogether. A later Evangelical bishop remarked:

> There was a sense of being beleaguered within a Church that seemed to be dominated by non-evangelicals. It was inevitable that there was to some extent a hard edge and a distrust of all who did not share what we felt to be the only expression of the truth.

Division over matters of scriptural interpretation was keenly felt among students. The influential Cambridge inter-collegiate

Christian Union disaffiliated from the Student Christian Movement in 1910, requiring 'first and final reference to the authority of Holy Scripture as its inerrant guide in all matters concerned with faith and morals'. As the century progressed, 'Conservative Evangelicalism' became an important feature of student religion, leading to the Inter-Varsity Fellowship.

A similar split occurred in 1922 in the Church Missionary Society (CMS). Things had been growing tense for a number of years – Anglo-Catholics had been asked to speak at some of the Society's meetings and a sub-committee had proposed co-operation with other missionary organizations. It was even suggested that candidates for the mission field should subscribe simply to a minimal statement of faith. This provoked bitter disagreement, with about 30 clergy and laity led by H. E. Fox, former Secretary of the CMS, setting up the *Bible* Churchmen's Missionary Society. A strong statement of Evangelical faith was produced. Alongside the belief that 'Scripture is the unerring Revelation of God, the one Rule of Faith, and the final Court of Appeal', they also required of their missionaries the

> belief that the theories of Sacerdotalism concerning the mechanical conveyance of grace in Baptism, Confirmation, the Supper of the Lord, and Ordination, whether these be professed in doctrine or implied in ritual, are 'grounded upon no warranty of Scripture, but, rather, are repugnant to the Word of God'.

Shortly afterwards, the veteran Archdeacon Mackay of Saskatchewan began work among the Inuit peoples. Before long there were BCMS missionaries in Burma and Africa. A college was set up in Bristol in 1925 for the training of missionaries, which became Tyndale Hall theological college in 1952.

Polarization affected the Evangelical theological colleges, with some, such as Ridley Hall, moving in a more open direction, and others adopting strongly conservative views. J. Stafford Wright,

Principal of Tyndale Hall, for instance, thought Barthianism (hardly a liberal trend) to be nothing more than a 'newer liberalism'.

Evangelicals triumphant

The turning point for Evangelicals in the 20th century came in the mid-1960s. In 1967, the chairman of the Islington Clergy Conference, a major gathering of Evangelicals, called for an end to isolation:

> The Church of England is changing. Indeed, it is in a state of ferment – although it remains to be seen whether ferment will result in mature vintage. On the other hand, Evangelicals in the Church of England are changing too. Not in doctrinal conviction (for the truth of the gospel cannot change), but (like any healthy child) in stature and posture. It is a tragic thing, however, that Evangelicals have a very poor image in the Church as a whole. We have acquired a reputation for narrow partisanship and obstructionism. We have to acknowledge this, and for the most part we have no one but ourselves to blame. We need to repent and to change. As for partisanship, I for one desire to be rid of all sinful 'party spirit'.

A similar attitude was adopted at the Keele Conference of the National Evangelical Anglican Council in 1967. Here there was the famous assertion of Anglican identity by John Stott (of All Souls', Langham Place) against Martin Lloyd-Jones' call for a new pan-Evangelical denomination. The result was increased commitment to changing the Church of England by entering into its structures and working with others. From the late 1960s, Evangelicals began to speak to others, moving out from their traditional centres, influencing the broader church. Others preferred the old ways and clubbed together in tight-knit campaigning groups with highly conservative views, particularly on Biblical interpretation, women's ordination, and homosexuality. The most influential have been Reform (founded in 1993), and the Proclamation Trust centred on St Helen's, Bishopsgate. Sometimes there have been messy splits, as with the divisions over the journal *Churchman* in 1982, which led to the setting up of *Anvil* as a more open alternative. A new group, 'Fulcrum', was set up in 2003, to provide a forum for more open Evangelicals.

Evangelicals like Julian Charley and George Carey, who became Archbishop of Canterbury through the 1990s, participated in ecumenical discussions. Many embraced liturgical renewal, as was evidenced by Colin Buchanan's important work for the *Alternative Service Book* of 1980. Nevertheless, at some points there was a refusal to budge. Keele upheld a strong line on baptism, siding with the traditional Evangelical requirement for conversion, at least among parents:

> Only the children of parents who profess to be Christians are fit subjects for this rite. Indiscriminate baptism, as commonly practised in England, is a scandal. . . . We must be welcoming to little children, as Jesus was. But we deny the propriety of baptizing the infants of parents who do not profess to be Christians themselves and who cannot promise to bring up their children as Christians.

Charismatic renewal

In the past 40 years or so, there have been significant influences from the Charismatic movement on Evangelicalism. It began in the American Episcopal Church on 3 April 1960 at St Mark's Church, Van Nuys, California, where the Rector, Dennis Bennett, experienced a revelation which divided the congregation. He moved to St Luke's, Seattle, where he continued to receive the gifts of the Spirit. The Holy Spirit moved to England in 1963, in Beckenham under George Forester, when a group of parishioners received a 'baptism in the Holy Spirit' (another expression for a conversion experience). Under the influence of such figures as Dick Watson in York and Michael Harper, this gradually came to be associated with a distinctive Christian counselling and healing ministry with a strongly dualistic emphasis on the battle between the forces of evil and good, which tended to see the world as dominated by principalities and powers. The effects of charismatic renewal are most obviously seen in the increasing informality of worship and hymns. The traditional Evangelical emphasis on the Prayer Book has been substituted in many churches by exuberant praise services, often coupled with a highly professional approach to communication and media. PowerPoint has replaced books.

Charismatic renewal has become a global phenomenon, establishing itself in a number of other Anglican provinces. It is frequently combined with conservative Biblical teaching. In South East Asia, Chiu Ban It, the first indigenous Bishop of Singapore, experienced the gifts of the Spirit in 1972, and this helped transform the approach of the diocese to worship. By 1974, weekly prayer and praise services had started at St Andrew's Cathedral. Bill Burnett, Archbishop of Cape Town, became a leader of charismatic renewal in southern Africa. Placing authority in the effects of the Holy Spirit, and emphasizing a second baptism in the Spirit, could be seen as a direct threat to the visible church – the old issues around the Gorham judgement have re-emerged in a quite different guise.

Recently, Evangelicals have been involved in modern arts festivals like Greenbelt, charismatic gatherings including New Wine, or more traditional rallies like Spring Harvest. Traditional Evangelical emphases, coupled with a strong sense of charismatic renewal, have found their way into the popular Christian multi-media initiation course, *Alpha*, produced by the English mega-church, Holy Trinity, Brompton, in the wealthiest part of central London. Built around a shared meal, it seeks to foster a sense of group belonging before 'marketing' its special product. Also important in urban areas have been 'church plants' which seek to transfer whole congregations and worship styles to declining churches, or to set up new churches in secular buildings.

There have been many other recent developments that have sought to stem the tide of decline in the Church of England, some of which have been pioneered elsewhere. These have been encouraged by the report *Mission Shaped Church*, which questions the relevance of the traditional geographical parochial system in a 'post-modern' context. New experiments with 'cell churches' and the 'Fresh Expressions' movement have tried to engage with sub-cultures and to move away from traditional patterns of belonging. Increasing fragmentation seems to be the future of English Evangelicalism. Globally, however, Evangelicalism is in the ascendant: from Singaporean charismatic renewal to Sydney's belligerent conservatism, a pan-Evangelicalism has become in some places as important as allegiance to Anglicanism. This has had a profound effect on the worldwide church.

Chapter 5
Anglo-Catholicism

Through its history Evangelicalism developed strong principles of boundary maintenance through group identity and partisan campaigns. In this it shares a great deal with the other great church party, 'Anglo-Catholicism', which developed out of the Oxford Movement of the 1830s and which defined itself over and against the groups of the wider church, sometimes 'evangelicals', sometimes 'liberals' (in their view, the real menace). Such a partisan identity displays the characteristics of a sect, understood sociologically. As one sympathetic writer claimed, Anglo-Catholicism was one of the 'sects' which comprised the Church of England, that 'microcosm' of the universal church. The term 'sect' provides a useful characterization of Anglo-Catholicism with its emphasis on holiness and authority: Anglo-Catholicism, like Evangelicalism, has been frequently reduced to a set of almost tribal identities or badges.

The religious revival that began in the 1830s among a group of young Oxford dons was caused by a complex set of ecclesiastical and political circumstances. Perhaps most important was the decreasing influence of the Church of England in the state, and the state's increasing reluctance to defend the church. Where kings (and parliaments) had once seen it as their duty to protect the church, it had become imperative for the church to defend itself. At its heart, the Oxford Movement was a response to a crisis in authority. If Evangelicalism had thrust the locus of authority from the monarch and the divinely appointed institutions of state to the experience of the individual heart and the truth of scripture, so the Oxford Movement sought to redirect authority towards a supernaturally ordered visible church.

In the years immediately preceding 1833, there were a number of specific 'attacks' on the Church of England. In 1828, the Test and Corporation Acts had been repealed, which meant that nonconformist men could hold public office and sit in Parliament. The following year saw the emancipation of Catholics, which led to significant opposition in Oxford to the University MP, Robert Peel, who had supported the Bill. Worse was to come in 1832 when a large number of middle-class men were enfranchised and many of the grossest abuses in the electoral system were reformed: new centres of power, possibly hostile to the church, were being created. The campaign to unseat Peel brought together an alliance of young men, principally associated with Oriel College, the intellectual powerhouse of the university. The Oxford Movement may have been centred on a small common room in a small college, but the impact on the wider church of conversations over buttered toast was profound.

To add insult to injury, the government sought to amalgamate a number of Irish bishoprics primarily on pragmatic grounds, since in parts of Ireland there were virtually no Anglicans. But there were higher principles at stake: what right had an assembly that now comprised dissenters and Roman Catholics to legislate in matters affecting the United Church of England and Ireland? How could successors of the apostles themselves be abolished by a human state? This led to John Keble's charge of National Apostasy in his sermon before the judges of the Oxford assizes in the University Church of 14 July 1833, which John Henry Newman marked as the beginning of the Oxford Movement: 'As a Christian nation she is also part of the Christian Church, and in all her legislation and policy bound by the fundamental rules of the church.' The 1833 measure was an outrageous affront to the rights of the church, a society 'built upon the Apostles and prophets, Jesus Christ himself being the chief corner stone'. If the state was no longer to defend the church, the logic ran, then it was the duty of the church to defend itself.

The doctrine of ministry and sacraments became central to the teachings of the Oxford Movement. Shortly after the Assize sermon, Newman (Figure 10) published the first of the *Tracts for the Times* (hence the alternative name 'Tractarian').

THE REV. MR. NEWMAN.

10. John Henry Newman was the first leader of the Tractarians

If the ministerial commission does not come from government, Newman asked, then where does it come from? The answer was from God himself. No gates of hell, not even a Whig government, could ever prevail against this sort of authority. As Henry Manning put it in 1835: 'The invisible spiritualities of our apostolical descent, and our ministerial power in the word and sacraments, no prince, no potentate, no apostate nation can sully with a breath of harm.' This extraordinary emphasis on the authority of the ministry led one outside observer to ask 'whether at any time in the history of the church the office of bishop has been so immoderately exalted to the clouds as in these early tracts'.

This high doctrine of the ministry led to a new sense of seriousness and a high view of the sacraments. Keble made it clear, on the grounds of apostolic succession, that the Church of England was 'the only church in this realm which has a right to be quite sure that she has the Lord's Body to give to his people'. The Tractarians thereby gained the confidence to face up to the threats on the church from both the state and competing forces within the church. They organized opposition to liberals, especially R. D. Hampden on his nomination as Regius Professor in 1836. Liberalism was a slippery slope which would lead to the dismemberment of the church. The church needed to assert its supernatural and divinely founded identity against all comers. Initially there was a great deal of common ground with other churchmen and few direct assaults on the Reformation. By the late 1830s, however, things began to change. Keble wrote in 1836: 'Anything which separates the present Church from the Reformers I should hail as a great good', and Hurrell Froude's (1803–36) posthumously published *Remains* was notorious for its anti-Reformation polemic.

Some Tractarians compared the nominal Christianity of the state church with the 'real' church established on the apostles. As Froude declared in an aphorism: 'Let us tell the truth and shame the devil; let us give up a national church and have a real one.'

John Henry Newman: Tract One on Ministerial Authority

Should the government and country so far forget their God as to cast off the church, to deprive it of its temporal honours and substance, on what will you rest the claim of respect and attention which you make upon your flocks? Hitherto you have been upheld by your birth, your education, your wealth, your connections; should these secular advantages cease, on what must Christ's ministers depend? . . .

There are some who rest their divine mission on their own unsupported assertion; others, who rest it on their popularity; others on their success; and others, who rest it on their temporal distinctions. The last case has, perhaps, been too much our own; I fear we have neglected the real ground on which our authority is built . . . our apostolical descent . . . We have been born, not of blood, nor of the will of the flesh, nor of the will of man, but of God. The Lord JESUS CHRIST gave His Spirit to His Apostles; they in turn laid their hands on those who would succeed them; and these again on others and so the sacred gift has been handed down to our present bishops, who have appointed us as their assistants, and in some sense representatives . . . We must necessarily consider none to be ordained who have not been thus ordained . . . Exalt our Holy Fathers the Bishops, as the Representatives of the Apostles, and the Angels of the Churches; and magnify your office, as being ordained by them to take part in their ministry.

Newman similarly sought to return power to the church. He turned round Henry VIII's argument: the church's powers had been usurped by a state, and a utilitarian and liberal state to boot. He wrote to Froude: 'The King . . . has literally betrayed us . . . Our first duty is the defence of the Church. We have stood by Monarchy and Authority till they have refused to stand by themselves.' While this could lead in the direction of disestablishment – and some, perhaps including Keble, seemed inclined to move in this direction – it would be fairer to see the Tractarians (like the puritans) as preferring a theocracy where the church, since it possessed the absolute truth, could dictate to the state.

There were obvious continuities with the past: there was a revival of interest in the 17th-century divines and their High Church successors who had emphasized the doctrine of apostolic succession. Their works were republished in the multi-volume *Library of Anglo-Catholic Theology*. However, where earlier Anglican theories of apostolic succession placed equal emphasis on the supernatural authority of the King, this was no longer possible for the Tractarians. Newman wrote to H. J. Rose in 1836: 'The single difference between their views [i.e. the Caroline Divines] and those I seem to follow is this – they had a divine right king – we in matter of fact have not.' Like many of their High Church predecessors, the Tractarians sought to defend their understanding of the church in the writings of the early Fathers, sponsoring a massive project of translation, *The Library of the Fathers*. It was the undivided church of the first centuries that provided their model of authentic Christianity.

The final Tract (XC) set the country ablaze. Newman had tried to offer a 'catholic' interpretation of the Thirty-Nine Articles. Most notorious was his defence of Article XXII on purgatory: it was, he claimed, only the *Romish* doctrine that was condemned. For Newman, this marked the beginning of the end of his association with the Church of England, with its 'indifference and scepticism' among those who 'are deficient in clear views of the truth'. There was little holding the Church of England together.

Rebuilding the church

The main focus of the Tractarians had been the advocacy of a distinctive theology of ministry which magnified the priestly office. From the late 1830s, this was to have a profound effect on the architecture and liturgy of the Church of England. Of vital importance was the Cambridge Camden Society, which spawned the so-called Ecclesiological Movement. Influenced by Pugin's polemics against the degenerate architecture of classicism, they sought to return the church to the true principles of Christian architecture. They set about describing the 'mutilated architectural remains' of English churches, as well as coming up with bold and somewhat dictatorial designs for rebuilding. In a time of rapid demographic change and expansion, both at home and overseas, such ideas could attract a quite disproportionate influence. They soon attracted a powerful following: by 1843 the Society had 18 bishops, and 31 peers or MPs among a membership of 700.

Many dioceses set up societies to promote architecture and ritual. The Exeter Architectural Society, for instance, would 'willingly sanction and, as far as their calling will permit, heartily abet every effort to make men good ritualists, sound churchmen and true men'. The physical appearance of churches was transformed: the focus moved from nave to chancel transforming the theology of both sacrament and word. The clergy were separated and elevated above their congregation. The favouring of the high medieval art of the 14th century led to a complete transformation of church interiors. Most importantly, there was a wholesale removal of furniture which had been constructed for the Book of Common Prayer. There were polemics against rented pews and their replacement with free benches. All people were equal in the sight of God – and all were to be given a view of the altar.

A great deal of energy was expended on cataloguing abuses. At Lenton in Nottinghamshire, for example, there was a 'w.c. contiguous to the Holy Altar itself, nay occupying a place where the Altar ought to stand. . . . We cannot trust ourselves to speak in sufficiently strong terms against this desecration of God's house.' The Camden Society decreed instead that the altar should be raised on a few steps above the height of the chancel; the font should be at the west end; hassocks were recommended in preference to boards; galleries were banned. Before long, organs began to replace parish bands. Everything in the church was to symbolize something: the tiles on the roof, for instance, were 'the soldiers, who preserve the church . . . from enemies'. This provoked a holy war against whitewash. When the clergyman set about restoring his church (and it seems nearly always to have proceeded in this direction) he was told to begin with the east end, traditionally the incumbent's responsibility. The Ecclesiologists sought to revitalize 'the principles which, it was supposed, guided medieval builders'. They protested 'against the merely business-like spirit of the modern profession' of architects, requiring instead 'the deeply religious habits of the builders of old' which had been perverted by 'worldliness, vanity and dissipation'.

Some new churches provoked considerable reaction, primarily because of the ritualism which accompanied the new designs. For instance, St Saviours, Leeds, founded by Pusey, was staffed by an unmarried 'college' of priests who started wearing Roman liturgical vestments as well as birettas. In 1850, St Barnabas, Pimlico, introduced an eagle lectern as well as banners, screens, and a cross and candles on the altar. This provoked one of the first great ritualist court cases: in the ruling altar lights were banned.

Most important of all the new churches was All Saints', Margaret Street, London (Figure 11) by William Butterfield. The dedication was chosen because it was easier to make pictures of lots of saints than to concentrate on the life of one saint. At the consecration of the new polychromatic church, Bishop Tait of London reminded the

11. 'A Model Ecclesiological Church': All Saints', Margaret Street, London, by William Butterfield

congregation that 'no church allows for such diversity of doctrine as the Church of England'. Nevertheless, the altar frontal had to be removed before the consecration and a table cloth hurriedly obtained. The Ecclesiologists were pleased with Butterfield's work:

> We do not say that All Saints', Margaret Street, is a perfect 'model church'. We have not scrupled here, as always, to criticize freely. But we assert, without fear of contradiction, that our generation has seen no greater or more memorable work, or one more pregnant with important consequences for the future of art in England.

Ritualism and reaction

Given the emphasis on ritual and the authority of the priest, it is hardly surprising that demarcation from other Anglicans was a concern of the Anglo-Catholics from the outset. Matters that in themselves were of little significance – such as the placing of flowers on the altar, or the abbreviation of saint to S. rather than St – could provoke vigorous reaction. The English Church Union was set up in 1859 to defend ritualists, affording 'counsel and protection to all persons, lay or clerical, suffering under unjust aggression or hindrance in spiritual matters'. By 1857, the following had already been declared legal: the credence table, the cross on the chancel screen, the unrestricted use of the cross as a symbol, frontals of various colours, and the altar cross as long as it was not fixed. What they lost were the stone altar covered with a lace cloth, and the permission to omit the inscription of the Ten Commandments from the chancel.

Many Evangelical MPs and churchmen became almost fixated on opposition to what they regarded as Anglican imitations of Rome. Lord Shaftesbury, for instance, lampooned the worship at A. H. Mackonochie's notorious ritualist church, St Alban's, Holborn:

> In outward form and ritual, it is the worship of Jupiter and Juno. . . .
> [It was] such a scene of theatrical gymnastics, and singing, screaming, genuflections, such strange movements of the priests, their backs almost always to the people, as I never saw before even in a Romish temple. . . . The communicants went up to the tune of soft music, as though it had been a melodrama, and one was astonished, at the close, that there was no fall of the curtain.

This defensive attitude led to the formation of the Church Association in 1865, which spent £40,000 prosecuting ritualists between 1868 and 1880.

Mackonochie was taken to court in 1867 for the use of incense and altar lights, and also for what was quaintly termed 'excessive kneeling'. The court cases led to rulings which reveal an extraordinary level of anxiety among Evangelicals. In 1870, the mixed chalice, wafers, the old eucharistic vestments of chasubles and tunicles were declared legal, but this was later overturned on appeal in 1871. Flower vases were legalized in 1870, although altar lights had to wait until 1890 to be lit. A Royal Commission led to Disraeli's 1874 Public Worship Regulation Act which, trying to outlaw the activities of ritualists, served to create 'martyrs' of those who were prosecuted. 'Father' Tooth of Hatcham and several others were imprisoned in 1877. In 1875, the ECU, under the influence of C. L. Wood (later Lord Halifax), adopted a manifesto of six points for which it was prepared to fight (the use of vestments, altar lights, the mixed chalice, wafer bread, incense, and facing east during the prayer of consecration, rather than standing at the north end as suggested in the Prayer Book). While none was regarded as a matter of faith, they were nonetheless elevated into matters of principle. The futility of the anti-ritualist stand became most evident in the campaign of 1888 against the ritualist Bishop Edward King of Lincoln, who was tried before Archbishop Benson, but, since he was a man of undoubted sanctity, the effect was to make the opponents look petty and narrow-minded.

Like Evangelicalism, Anglo-Catholicism was marked by a strong sense of identity. Certain symbols or practices (such as sacramental confession or ritualized ablutions) became the outward signs of belonging. Often bizarre societies devoted to practices like adoration of the blessed sacrament or prayers for the dead became markers of group identity. Most influential was the Society of the Holy Cross, founded in 1855 by Charles Lowder, which mimicked the missionary orders of the Roman Church. Calls for 'retreats', together with devotional manuals with a Roman pedigree, invited denunciations from politicians and churchmen alike. At St George's in the East in London, Lowder famously sought to minister to both the spiritual and social needs of the people, but was quickly subjected, as one observer noted, to a barrage of criticism from 'publicans and brothel-keepers' who were fighting our Lord 'with the weapons of Protestantism'. Bishop Tait soon withdrew his opposition as he felt that the good Lowder was doing for the poor far outweighed the harm of ritualism.

A strong sense of identity spilled over into a total vision of life, particularly among the clergy. Bishop Samuel Wilberforce wrote of the ritualist students at his own theological college at Cuddesdon near Oxford. He considered:

> it a heavy affliction that they should wear neckcloths of particular construction, coats of peculiar cut, whiskers of peculiar dimensions – that they should walk with a peculiar step, carry their heads at a peculiar angle to the body, and read in a peculiar tone.

Men like Pusey and the Ecclesiologist J. M. Neale were responsible for encouraging the revival of the religious life, particularly among women. This proved extraordinarily successful: by 1900 there were around 10,000 members of religious orders in England, nearly all strongly influenced by ritualism. For the first time since the Reformation, Anglican women could become religious 'professionals', even if the question of ordination was not addressed.

Broad churchmen

There were, of course, many churchmen through the 19th century who were neither Evangelicals nor Anglo-Catholics. They were often labelled 'Broad Churchmen' and associated with the new 'public' schools. Many, including the leading theologian F. D. Maurice, disliked the 'new nickname' because it suggested that they were merely another party. He attacked the notion of party in the name of a broad national church, whose boundaries should be co-terminous with those of the state. 'The Church exists', he wrote, 'to tell the world of its true Centre, of the law of mutual sacrifice by which its parts are bound together. The Church exists to maintain the order of the nation and the order of the family.' Many, like Dean

A. P. Stanley of Westminster Abbey, came under the influence of Thomas Arnold, headmaster of Rugby, who sought to educate his boys in the pursuit of truth as they matured from boyhood to manhood. Another influence was the poet-philosopher Samuel Taylor Coleridge, 'in whom', according to Julius Hare, one of the leading theologians of the time, 'practical judgement and moral dignity and a sacred love of truth are so nobly wedded to the highest intellectual power'. Much survived of their national church ideal into the 20th century. It proved vitally important in times of national crisis and in the building up of the welfare state.

The Oxford professor Benjamin Jowett was a key contributor to *Essays and Reviews* (1860), the most important broad church publication. His essay on 'The Interpretation of Scripture' challenged Evangelicals and Anglo-Catholics alike with the view that the Bible should be treated like any other book. Another author, Frederick Temple, who went on to become Archbishop of Canterbury, wrote: 'If the conclusions are prescribed, the study is precluded.' Despite frequent controversy, the influence of such figures was profound in gaining acceptance of critical thought and in ensuring that the church remained a credible intellectual force. Even among Anglo-Catholics, there was an increasing acceptance of critical scholarship, particularly after the publication in 1889 of another collected work, *Lux Mundi*, edited by Charles Gore, first Principal of Pusey House, Oxford, and a future Bishop, whom some regarded as betraying Pusey's legacy. For other churchmen from both Anglo-Catholic and Evangelical parties, however, critical thought remained anathema.

Anglo-Catholicism in the 20th century

In the later years of the 19th century, Anglo-Catholicism grew rapidly. Ritualism began to cross over from the partisan extremes into the mainstream of Church of England life. At the same time, a number of influential Anglo-Catholics were appointed to the episcopate. However, like Evangelicalism, Anglo-Catholicism began to fragment into different groups by the turn of the 20th century. Different styles of dress, coupled with the intricacies of liturgy and ritual, became identifiers of particular *varieties* of ritualism or catholicism: what was called the 'Sarum Empire' (after the reverence for the 1549 Prayer Book with its remnant of medieval ritual) was pitched against the forces of the quasi-Romanists. Although the extraordinary achievement of the ritualists had left virtually no church building untouched by the Gothic revival, which meant that worship, even in country parishes, was almost unrecognizably different from 70 years before, most Church of England people and clergy would have been reluctant to identify themselves as Anglo-Catholic. Perhaps the greatest liturgical achievement was the rise of the Parish Communion movement, especially after the Second World War, which established the eucharist as the main Sunday service in probably the majority of English churches. The name 'Anglo-Catholic', however, was reserved for those who followed a distinctive set of practices, art, and dress. Roughly speaking, there were two main trajectories of Anglo-Catholicism through the 20th century. One of these – which might be referred to as 'English Catholicism' – moved into the Anglican mainstream. The other strand, which will be discussed first, was associated with the fashionable extremism of an alternative and often very precisely defined culture.

The exotic and the aesthetic: counter-cultural extremism

That ecclesiastical 'naughtiness' which had hitherto characterized only a few of the more 'advanced' Romanizers of the urban slums spread widely in the years before the First World War. An odd but explosive mixture of baroque aestheticism and anti-authoritarianism found expression in a small but influential group that gathered around a church-furnishing shop. Under the inspiration of Ronald Knox (son of an Evangelical bishop) and Maurice Child, the 'Society of SS. Peter and Paul' established itself (in a less than modest claim) as 'Publishers to the Church of

England', promoting Roman liturgical practice. They produced ecclesiastical, liturgical, and satirical pamphlets, often with baroque decoration, 'to be sold at half-price to bishops and deans'. Caution was cast aside in favour of the quixotic and downright frivolous.

Child offended the sensibilities of more sensitive churchmen with advertisements in the *Church Times* for 'Latimer and Ridley Candle Stands'. Knox's appearance must have been equally shocking: cassock, silk stockings, and buckled shoes, to which he added 'a quite new sartorial outrage in the name of a mantelletta'. There was, as Evelyn Waugh pointed out, the 'touch of the dandy about him'. With destructive and acerbic wit, he denounced anything that did not conform to his style of aesthetic religion.

The love of the extreme extended into the baroque church décor of Martin Travers and the ordering of liturgy, with parishes attempting to be more Roman than the Romans. Some introduced 'High Mass' in which the congregation did not receive communion, held regular 'private' masses for particular intentions, and adopted Latin practices such as the stations of the cross and use of the rosary. Much of this was done in flagrant disobedience to episcopal authority. Pilgrimage re-established itself, particularly after the restoration of the Shrine of 'Our Lady' at 'England's Nazareth' at Walsingham in Norfolk, which became the centre of an extraordinary combination of English romantic medievalism and post-Tridentine Latin Christianity. Organizations established themselves devoted to reconciliation with Rome, one of them (the Catholic League) explicitly accepting and praying for the Bishop of Rome.

Consistency was never the hallmark of this style of Anglo-Catholicism. While it elevated the doctrine of bishops, it usually practised the most extreme form of congregationalism. Outwardly it could maintain a strong moral line, while at the same time becoming a safe haven for homoeroticism, a trait notoriously (if implausibly) identified by Geoffrey Faber even in the Oxford Apostles themselves. As Evelyn Waugh wrote somewhat crudely in *Brideshead Revisited*: 'beware of the Anglo-Catholics – they're all sodomites with unpleasant accents'.

English Romantic Catholicism

This strange amalgam of sexuality, Romanism, and a sectarian mentality was not, however, the only strand of Anglo-Catholic church life through the 20th century. Another strand was developed by Percy Dearmer, incumbent of St Mary's Church, Primrose Hill, in north London. A student of art and liturgy, Dearmer published the *Parson's Handbook* in 1899, an extraordinarily influential manual of English liturgical practice. Drawing on English historical resources, his style of Catholicism was derided by opponents as 'British Museum Religion'. Following the example of the Romantic socialists, especially William Morris and John Ruskin, he sought to integrate life and art in what has been called 'sacramental socialism'. Along with the composer Ralph Vaughan Williams, Dearmer edited the *English Hymnal* which drew widely from the English folk tradition. The book was inspired by a great sense of duty. In the preface Dearmer wrote:

> The great hymns, indeed, of all ages abound in the conviction that duty lies at the heart of the Christian life – a double duty to God and to our neighbour; and such hymns, like the Prayer Book, are for all sorts and conditions of men.

Dearmer's manual was based on the ornaments rubric of the Prayer Book, with its injunction to do things as they were done in the second year of the reign of Edward VI. Cathedrals and parish churches throughout the country were challenged to redesign altars and church furnishings on the late medieval pattern, ensuring that everything was as it had been before the Elizabethan rot set in. Dearmer became the great choreographer of the Prayer Book, and his architectural suggestions were executed lavishly by Ninian

Comper, the designer of numerous gilded angels set on riddell · posts. Dearmer's historical myth proved deeply influential on the ceremonial and layout of churches: it amounts to a practical expression of a reformed Catholicism but one deeply permeated by English nationalism. It created a form of Anglo-Catholicism that was far more 'Anglo' than 'Catholic'.

Triumphant Anglo-Catholicism

After the First World War, Anglo-Catholicism appeared triumphant. Many of the ritualist battles had been won (or at least bishops had been ignored). In Rose Macaulay's novel *Dangerous Ages* (1921), Grandmamma asks: '"Who *are* these Anglo-Catholics, my dear? One seems to hear so much of them in these days. I can't help thinking they are rather *noisy*", as she might have spoken of Bolshevists, or the Labour Party, or Sinn Fein'. A noisy group with strange practices made a mark far beyond the sectarian confines of earlier partisan movements. Although there are no accurate figures, a common estimate for 1930 is that about one-third of all Church of England priests and lay communicants identified themselves as Anglo-Catholics: where Evangelicalism was divided, Anglo-Catholicism appeared to be victorious.

The first Anglo-Catholic Congress was held in 1920. It proved to be far more popular than any of its planners had expected. The queues for the opening service at Southwark extended across the River Thames. Its leadership was provided by Frank Weston, the dynamic and charismatic Bishop of Zanzibar. Three years later another Congress was held at the Albert Hall, attended by about 2,000 clergy and 13,000 laity, but with only two English bishops. Weston dominated the proceedings. His famous closing speech sent shock waves through the Church of England, partly on account of his notorious defence of tabernacles (where the blessed sacrament was reserved on the altar for the purposes of adoration), but also because of his radical social conscience:

You cannot claim to worship Jesus in the tabernacle if you do not pity Jesus in the slum. . . . It is folly, it is madness, to suppose that you can worship Jesus in the sacrament and Jesus on the throne of glory when you are sweating Him in the bodies and souls of his children.

Although Weston was subjected to a barrage of criticism for his partisan extremism, his radical social vision was far removed from the aestheticism of the Society of SS. Peter and Paul.

Following these congresses, Anglo-Catholicism spread into the parishes through its publishing and educational work. At the same time, it grew as a serious intellectual force under such theologians as Kenneth Kirk and N. P. Williams, and as a social force through the Schools of Sociology and the Christendom Group. By 1927, a Eucharistic Congress had been held and three years later 'High Mass' was celebrated before 18,000 at Chelsea football ground: it looked as though the Anglo-Catholic party had achieved a lasting victory. Yet there was no obvious leader to succeed Weston after his death in 1925; in 1930 not a single English diocesan bishop was present at the Congress. There were few who could command Weston's respect: most were either too cautious or too radical to be acceptable outside the party camp.

Anglo-Catholicism and the future

That brief period of success, however, was uncharacteristic of a movement that had traditionally courted controversy and defined itself negatively against a common (although often imaginary) foe; at one time, this was Modernism as displayed in the controversies over the publication of *Foundations* in 1912; at another, it was Ecumenism (at least with non-episcopal churches), as demonstrated by Weston over the Kikuyu Missionary Conference and later over the South India Scheme; most recently, many Anglo-Catholics have set themselves against the ordination of women. Like some factions within Evangelicalism, many

Anglo-Catholics have defined themselves negatively against the wider church with its so-called 'liberal' agenda.

In the contemporary Church of England, partisan Anglo-Catholicism can seem like a movement that has lost its direction. *New Directions*, the publication of Forward in Faith, the Anglo-Catholic group organized for those opposed to the ordination of women, comes over as a sad, bitter, and defensive magazine. Such an attitude has not proved popular: no more than a couple of hundred parishes have opted for 'extended episcopal oversight' (see Chapter 7). Where Evangelicalism flourishes in parishes and attracts increasing numbers, Anglo-Catholicism is declining.

That said, the more inclusive strand of Anglo-Catholicism that followed in the direction pioneered by Gore and Dearmer (who drew on the legacy of the broad churchman F. D. Maurice) found its way into mainstream Anglicanism through the liturgical renewal of the 1960s and 1970s. It began to dominate the theological approach of those in positions of authority. Decried by many Anglo-Catholics as liberals, Archbishops Michael Ramsey and Robert Runcie both came from an open Anglo-Catholic background. Rowan Williams, Archbishop of Canterbury from 2002, also comes from this tradition, but is far too subtle and creative a thinker to be identified with parties. He was one of the founders of 'Affirming Catholicism', a group of Anglo-Catholics in favour of the ordination of women and far less sectarian in its approach. Whether contemporary Anglicanism has much space for such subtlety remains an open question.

Chapter 6
The global communion

Earlier chapters have shown the Church of England to be based on a theory of royal supremacy. Ordination oaths were (and still are) sworn to a monarch who was also supreme governor of the church, but over which Parliament had become increasingly sovereign. This meant that the church was subject to predominantly lay control, even though the bishops had a constitutional right to sit in the House of Lords. The Church of England was so tied up with the state that it was far from clear what it could possibly mean outside England. The word 'Anglican' is little more than a Latinized form of 'English' (and was used in conscious imitation of 'Gallican' as the French equivalent). Henry VIII's theory of ecclesiastical autonomy means that decisions were often made with scant regard to other churches: all sovereignty over both church and state was to be exercised within national boundaries. As the Church of England expanded overseas, it became clear that something different would have to emerge: could there be an Anglicanism where the King of England was not sovereign? What would be the role of local legislatures in regulating a church whose final authority depended on the British Parliament?

It comes as little surprise that questions about the nature of Anglicanism emerged through the 19th century. Shorn of its political underpinning, was it simply a vague sense of Englishness in religion? As William Reed Huntington (1838–1909), Rector of

Grace Church, New York, asked: was it little more than the 'flutter of surplices, a vision of village spires and cathedral towers, a somewhat stiff and stately company of deans, prebendaries and choristers'? Or was there something else that constituted the essence of Anglicanism? Answers began to emerge, sometimes intentionally and sometimes quite accidentally, as new churches were established across the globe. At the same time, however, the different parties and groups which were growing simultaneously in England had quite distinct ideas about what the church should be like. Fundamental differences divided the parties in England; their competing visions exported overseas meant that the new churches sometimes encountered significant internal conflict and division.

The first independent churches: Scotland and America

The political problems of Anglicanism outside England can be glimpsed from as early as the 17th century. After the union of the English and Scottish crowns, for much of the 17th century there was a strange blend of bishops and Presbyterianism in Scotland. Yet after William III's seizure of power in 1688, the Scottish bishops refused to swear the oath of allegiance: throughout the 18th century there were questions of loyalty, and bishops were not officially tolerated until 1712. With many continuing to support Stuart claims, Scottish Episcopalian clergy were banned from officiating after the Jacobite rebellion of 1745. It was only in 1792, after the death of the last Stuart claimant, that the penal laws were eventually repealed. Nevertheless, Scottish clergy were not allowed to hold ecclesiastical positions in England. The Scottish Episcopal Church survived as an independent body, which for practical purposes was not 'in communion' with the Church of England. Indeed, the sense in which such a church can be called 'Anglican' is open to question. It was supported neither by Crown nor Parliament and had to find its authority elsewhere. It is no surprise that the Scottish Episcopal Church was closely associated with the

Oxford Movement, with its high view of the independent authority of the church, almost from the beginning.

A different model is offered by the growth of chaplaincies at the various British trading stations that were set up from the beginning of the 17th century. It did not take long for chaplains to make the long journey to America and to plant churches. Virginia had adopted the English pattern, with parishes and churchwardens by 1630. Since there were no bishops, the Governor presented clergy to posts. In 1634, the Bishop of London was given responsibility for English congregations overseas, although it was highly unlikely he would find time to visit them. Shortly before the English Civil War, Laud had tried to organize a scheme to appoint a bishop to North America that came to nothing. After his appointment to London in 1675, Henry Compton began to tidy up the oversight of overseas chaplains and to organize endowments; commissaries were appointed who frequently fell out with Governors. In practice, it was difficult to assert authority over individual congregations.

The most influential commissary of all was Thomas Bray, who was appointed to Maryland by Compton. He recognized the need for more organized work in the colonies, setting up the Society for Promoting Christian Knowledge (SPCK) in 1698 to encourage literature and education, and three years later the Society for the Propagation of the Gospel in Foreign Parts (SPG). Supported by leading English churchmen, they set about trying to appoint bishops for the colonies, as well as organizing missions to the unevangelized (the 'heathen' as they were known at the time). There was a desperate need for local organization: the 300 or so missionaries sent out to America before independence were far too distant to maintain any real sense of contact with the Bishop of London, and there was little hope of missionary activity without a ready supply of ministers: the journey to London for ordination was hardly an incentive for an increase in vocations. The weakness of central authority gave vestries much greater power than they had in England: in most colonies parish priests were appointed by parishioners, and churches became increasingly self-supporting.

The creation of bishops would have been likely to arouse the opposition of other denominations in America. The Stamp Act of 1765 had imposed a tax on the colonies without reference to their legislatures: it would be just as easy to impose establishment. In 1771, there was a successful lobby in London against a petition from New York and New Jersey to appoint a bishop. For bishops to succeed in North America would require a different model of episcopacy from that exercised by their English counterparts. The 'primitive' model would limit their authority solely to the spiritual realm, removing all trappings of political power. Some colonies were content to maintain the status quo, having grown used to freedom from episcopal interference; the legislature in Maryland even regarded bishops as unnecessary.

Matters had still not been settled in 1776 when the Declaration of Independence was signed. This created a new situation for the Church of England clergy ministering in America: would they continue to support the King and keep to their ordination oaths? Or would they declare their support for the new regime? Some travelled north to the loyalist colonies of Nova Scotia and New Brunswick, but others remained in the newly independent states. How an Anglican church could survive without a king or parliament, as one denomination among others, had to be quickly addressed before the supply of clergy dried up and the church collapsed.

Eventually the State Conventions discussed the oversight and relationships between the different congregations. While the role of laity was widely affirmed, there was a range of different opinions on the role of bishops. Congregational independence was highly prized. In 1783 the clergy of Connecticut nominated Samuel Seabury (Figure 12), a loyal supporter of Britain during the War of Independence, to be consecrated bishop.

12. Samuel Seabury, first bishop of the American Episcopal Church

In the summer of 1783, he arrived in England seeking ordination –
the English bishops declined since they did not wish to be seen to be
interfering in another sovereign country, and he would not be able
to make the statutory oath. An alternative solution had to be
sought. The Scottish bishops were approached and consecrated
him in November 1784, despite the fact that their relationship with
the English Church was far from cordial. When news reached
America, representatives from other states agreed a draft
constitution for a General Convention comprising clergy and laity

which proposed a bishop for every state. The name 'Protestant Episcopal Church' was adopted. It was intended that the church would keep as close as possible to the doctrines and rites of the Church of England.

Seabury did not attend the next Convention in 1785 in case his authority was not recognized. There were disagreements as to the role of the laity and the state convention in the nomination of bishops. The following year, William White, chaplain of the Continental Congress, and Samuel Provoost of Trinity Church, New York, were elected as candidates for bishops. This time they were presented to the Archbishop of Canterbury by John Adams, the American minister in London, who assured him that the consecration would not be regarded as interfering in American political affairs. The necessary Act of Parliament was obtained, which meant that bishops could be ordained without swearing the oath of allegiance. Both were consecrated in February 1787 very soon after American Independence.

The role of bishops, however, was far from clear. Some states had failed to elect a bishop; Maryland suggested lay oversight. Eventually, however, there was agreement at the 1789 General Convention which allowed for a House of Deputies consisting of clergy and laymen and also a House of Bishops which could scrutinize and reject legislation. Canons were prepared and a liturgy approved. It was agreed that the Convention should meet every three years. A fourth bishop was consecrated for Virginia by the English bishops, and in 1792 the Bishop of Maryland was consecrated by the four American bishops. Given the wide range of opinions and long experience of virtual congregationalism, it was a triumph that agreement was reached.

Nevertheless, the American church had lost many thousands of members. In 1800 there were probably only about 12,000 communicants. Bishop Provoost resigned in 1801, convinced that the Episcopal Church would die out without the old colonial establishment. While influential and historical, it was also small and could not hope to resemble the national church ideal of the Church of England. Although it was not as weak as the Scottish Church, it was simply one church among many. It developed in parallel to the Church of England: the partisan developments that affected England were not wholly shared by Americans. It took until 1840 before formal communion with the Church of England was established. The American democratic tradition coupled with a long legacy of self-supporting congregations has had repercussions on global Anglicanism up until the present day.

Canada

Things went very differently in Canada. In Nova Scotia the Church of England had been 'established' by the colonial legislature in 1758 but operated with SPG chaplains without a bishop. The Governor was 'directed to induct the minister' and 400 acres of land were set apart to support the clergyman. During the American War of Independence there was a significant influx of immigrants, including some disaffected clergy, from the former colonies. This meant that there was an urgent need for oversight. Pitt's government appointed a bishop for Nova Scotia who would also cover the territories of New Brunswick, Prince Edward Island, and Newfoundland. The aim in part was to ensure loyalty to the Crown. Charles Inglis, the Irish Rector of Trinity Church, New York, was appointed without reference to the colonies themselves. He was consecrated by Archbishop Moore in 1787, returning to take charge of a church of 11 clergy. With grants from the SPG, in the hands of an influential group of High Churchmen, the Hackney Phalanx, the church expanded rapidly, but from the outset there were difficulties with the civil authorities. Inglis was not the easiest character: he was not much given to travel, which did not go down well in such a vast diocese. Parliament in Britain, however, continued to support the church in Canada. By 1816, the relationships between church and state were so close that the chaplain (Robert Stanser) to the House of Assembly was recommended to succeed Inglis as bishop.

In 1793, a separate diocese of Quebec was formed, with Jacob Mountain, Vicar of St Andrew's, Norwich, as first bishop. He imported the organist from Norwich cathedral and employed a surpliced choir at his own expense: the Church of England was being planted in unfamiliar territory. Establishment, however, did not last: the Church of England was only a minority church. In England it became increasingly difficult to justify parliamentary favouritism for an overseas church, particularly after the repeal of the Test and Corporation Acts in 1828 and Catholic Emancipation the following year. Mountain's successor, Charles James Stewart, worked far more closely with other Protestant denominations. Resentment over the land reserved to finance clergy reached a peak in the 1830s and was one of the chief causes of the rebellion in 1837 in Upper Canada. Two years later, the land reserves were sold with the proceeds going to religious causes.

In the 1830s, SPG grants were reduced, coming to an end in 1839, and in 1851 the new Bishop of Nova Scotia, Hibbert Binney, was refused a seat in the legislative assembly. Six years later, John Medley, Bishop of Fredericton in New Brunswick, resigned his seat, which marked an end to Anglican establishment. From then on, the Church in Canada would have to support itself, competing on a level playing field with the other denominations. John Inglis, who had followed his father as Bishop of Nova Scotia, formed 'Church Societies' to raise money to supplement and eventually replace the SPG funds. In Newfoundland, despite harsh climatic conditions, Edward Feild, Bishop from 1844, worked energetically to build a cathedral and a theological college.

Following the Quebec Conference in 1851, synods were formed and from 1861 Canada was constituted a separate province. A General Synod met in 1893 which affirmed the desire to remain in communion with the Church of England throughout the world. Identity was to be conferred through the use of the Prayer Book and the Thirty-Nine Articles. The form of Anglicanism that developed in Canada was far closer to that of England than in the United

States: bishops came and went between Britain and Canada; conflicts emerged between Tractarians and Evangelicals: in Toronto, Evangelicals founded what became Wycliffe College, in competition to Trinity College, which had come under high church influence. Yet there were crucial differences: as in the USA, so in Canada the Anglican Church became one denomination among many. Its numbers were relatively modest, especially compared to Roman Catholics, who constituted nearly half the population.

India and Australasia

The expansion of the Church of England into the East took a quite different course. From 1698, the East India Company was required to provide chaplains to its trading stations, who had to learn local languages. During the 18th century, the SPCK worked to encourage education among Indians, and, since it could not persuade English clergy to go to India, worked closely with missionaries from Germany and Denmark. By the beginning of the 19th century, the Church Missionary Society, founded by members of the Clapham Sect in 1799, sought to engage with the indigenous population. Claudius Buchanan had been deeply influenced by Henry Thornton and began a chaplaincy to India in 1797. He sketched out a proposal for a bishop for India which came to fruition under William Wilberforce's influence, with the consecration of Thomas Middleton as first Bishop of Calcutta in 1814. He was closely associated with Joshua Watson and the High Churchmen of the Hackney Phalanx. His primary intention was to serve the English settlers rather than to convert the local population: 'My public reception was certainly so arranged as not to alarm the natives.' His diocese included not merely India, but also Ceylon, Penang, and Australia. Relations with the Governor General were frosty: Middleton believed in raising up a local clergy capable of relating to the dominant Hindu culture, whereas the Company sought to exercise control over its chaplains.

By 1817, the SPG had decided to redirect its energies to the East.

Together with large grants from the SPCK and the CMS this meant that a training College for missionaries could be established. Conflict between the missionary societies soon developed. The CMS proved reluctant to have its missionaries accountable to a bishop whom they regarded as holding dubious opinions. The bishop was also unsure about whether his letters patent allowed him to ordain local missionaries. This situation was clarified in 1823 when an Act of Parliament allowed for Middleton's successor, Reginald Heber, to ordain Indian clergy. Conflict continued between the missionary societies: the SPG was happy to allow the bishop to organize missionary work, whereas the CMS preferred direct control of its missionaries. Heber died suddenly in 1825 and was succeeded by the staunchly Evangelical Daniel Wilson, Vicar of Islington. Despite his background, however, conflict with the CMS continued until an uneasy agreement was reached in 1836. The question for the growth of independent dioceses was obvious: should the bishop disagree with the mission agency then who should have the final say?

Similar tensions emerged in the penal colony of New South Wales, established in 1788. Richard Johnson was licensed as chaplain to the settlement. In 1794, on Simeon's recommendation, he was joined by Samuel Marsden, who succeeded him in 1800. Marsden proved a disciplinarian magistrate, hardly likely to endear himself to his flock. Development was slow: by 1819 there were only four Anglican clergy in what had become an ill-governed colony. Things improved following the publication of a report in 1823 that established land endowments on the Canadian pattern. The church was organized as an Archdeaconry of the diocese of Calcutta in 1825, supported by the SPCK. William Grant Broughton (1788–1853), a friend of Joshua Watson and the Duke of Wellington, was appointed Archdeacon in 1829. He was consecrated the first (and only) Bishop of Australia in 1836 with a salary paid by the British government. However, as with Canada, government grants soon dried up and it proved impossible to establish the church on the English pattern. Relations with the Governor, Richard Bourke, were fraught. Fighting against the sectarianism that dogged his native Ireland, Bourke carried through the Church Acts (1836 and 1837), which allocated religious subsidies to Anglicans, Roman Catholics, Presbyterians, and Wesleyans. The terms were generous: within a year £23,000 had been collected. Parishes increased from 12 to 36, and work was begun on a cathedral. By 1847, the vast diocese was divided, with Broughton becoming Bishop of Sydney and Metropolitan of Australia.

During a visit to England from 1807 to 1809, the Australian chaplain, Marsden, persuaded the CMS to send a mission to New Zealand. By 1814, the Maori Chief Ruatara agreed to protect three missionaries. By 1830, there were 12 missionaries; 10 years later there were 30,000 Maoris taking part in public worship. Broughton visited New Zealand on behalf of the CMS in 1838–9, recognizing the need for more ordained men. The CMS supported the appointment of a bishop, and in 1840 a New Zealand Church Society was formed with the support of Lord John Russell, Secretary for the Colonies. The Treaty of Waitangi in 1841 established New Zealand as a colony in co-operation with the Maori population. George Augustus Selwyn (1809–78) arrived in New Zealand in 1842 as first Bishop. Half his salary was paid by the CMS, although they were not consulted on his appointment: relations between Selwyn, who had been deeply influenced by the Tractarians, and the CMS became increasingly strained. While supporting establishment in England, he sought a constitution for New Zealand which would allow clergy and laity to regulate their own affairs unfettered to the state. Supported by the colonial authorities, he completed a draft constitution for the Church of New Zealand in 1857, securing its adoption at the first general synod in 1859: the Church in New Zealand became a voluntary organization like its counterpart in Australia.

During a time in England before his consecration, Broughton came under the influence of the Tractarian understanding of independent ecclesiastical authority. To discuss the issue of political interference, Broughton invited the bishops of Australasia to Sydney in 1850 where a decision was made to introduce synodical government at a diocesan and provincial level: no rights were left with the Crown. Although there was opposition in Britain to synods, out of a fear that they might be dominated by men of dubious churchmanship, Broughton called for unilateral action to remove all legal obstacles. He asked the SPG to organize a meeting with colonial bishops from Canada and South Africa to draft a joint declaration to transfer all authority to the local churches. Broughton agreed to preside over the meeting and to draft a document calling either for re-establishment or for independence. He discussed his plans with Bishops Mountain and Gray of Cape Town but died before the conference could be convened. National and provincial synods were taken up enthusiastically in many provinces, although the Church of England remained opposed. A different version of Anglicanism emerged. The careful balance between lay control and episcopal authority pioneered by Selwyn in New Zealand provided a model for other provinces, even the Church of Ireland, which was finally severed from its links with the state in 1871.

'Colonial bishoprics' and the CMS

Samuel Wilberforce, who became Bishop of Oxford in 1845, had been one of the leading figures promoting the acceptance of the American Church in 1840: during his researches he came across the idea of the 'missionary bishop', developed by Bishop G. W. Doane of New Jersey in a sermon preached at the consecration of Jackson Kemper as Bishop of Missouri and Indiana. Bishops were seen less as overseers of pre-existing churches, and more as pioneer evangelists following the example of the early apostles. As Wilberforce put it in 1838: the task was 'to send out the Church, and not merely instructions about religion . . . this is the way in which in primitive times the church was converted'. The visible church in the person of the bishop was the first step rather than final task.

With the growth of Tractarianism in England, the idea of ecclesiastical independence under the leadership of bishops had became increasingly prominent. Charles Blomfield, Bishop of London, responsible for the Church overseas, published an open letter in 1840, in which he spoke of the need for 'the full benefits of her apostolical ordinances' throughout the British Empire. This led to the setting up of the Colonial Bishoprics' Fund in 1841, which raised huge sums of money and had set up 15 dioceses by 1853. Speaking of the fund, Henry Manning claimed: 'There has been no time when the Church of England stood stronger than now, in the apostolic doctrine and discipline.' As the examples of Australia and New Zealand show, such apostolic ideals were shared across the colonial churches. With the loss of government funding, self-government was both a practical necessity and a divine prerogative.

The CBF was closely aligned with the SPG, the largest contributor, and dominated by churchmen with a high view of episcopacy. The CMS was more ambivalent in its support. Henry Venn, secretary of the CMS, took the opposite view from Wilberforce and Blomfield. Churches should raise up clergy and leaders from within: they were to be national churches responsive to their local conditions and should seek civil protection from the colonial legislatures. Venn espoused what was called the 'three selfs' for local churches: self-extension, self-support, and self-governance. The principle was put clearly by Hugh Stowell in the CMS Annual Sermon of 1841: episcopacy 'ought not to anticipate but to follow evangelisation . . . it is when a country has been evangelised that the episcopate comes in, to crown and consummate the work'. For Wilberforce, Venn's system was simply a means by which the CMS would gain the upper hand of the bishops. He wrote to James Stephen, Venn's brother-in-law: 'Henry Venn is the autocrat of the CMS. He fears that missionary bishops would supersede Church missionary committees and his own secret power.'

The CMS, almost from its beginnings in 1799, worked in West Africa from the base of Sierra Leone. The few Europeans who had gone to West Africa (unlike South Africa) soon succumbed to illness, which meant it was imperative to provide an African leadership. A small group of well-educated local clergy, some of whom had adopted English names, were later to be central in the missionary movements along the Niger River. Many retained knowledge of their African language, which allowed them easier contact with the local population. Central to Venn's strategy of 'a native church under native pastors and a native episcopate' was Samuel Crowther (Figure 13), ordained in 1843, who opened the first mission station in the Niger Delta in 1845.

13. **Samuel Adjai Crowther, first black bishop in the Anglican Communion**

Progress was slow, but the policy gradually changed from the planting of small mission stations to that of 'native churches', which emerged from the bottom up. Venn sought what was called the 'euthanasia' of the mission and the 'full development of the native African church'. The CMS became a self-extending agency pushing out from its bases, although the model of the church adopted was still far from being fully inculturated. As one African critic put it:

> A critical defect within Venn's scheme ... was the fact that it proposed an indigenous church imprisoned within decidedly European patterns and expectations. The Church of the 'three-selfs' was envisioned as merely an extension or outpost of a European model, with no separate organic spiritual life of its own.

Crowther was consecrated bishop in 1864. Somewhat ironically, his diocese of the Niger was very much established on Wilberforce's missionary model. He was working in unfamiliar territory. The job he should have been doing – leading the Yoruba church – was being done by no one. The treatment of Crowther was often harsh, especially by missionaries who found it hard to accept the authority of an African. Some feared that it would be like 'giving school children control of their master'. Yet the success of the Niger Delta Pastorate was undeniable. With Crowther and others, including James Johnson, the precedent had been set: churches could raise their own clergy and might challenge the prevailing model. Even if Nigeria had to wait until 1952 for its next African bishop, this experience proved that a local elite could produce new varieties and adaptations of Christianity. In later generations an educated African leadership would frequently be caught between the competing demands of nationalism and Christianity. Hardly surprisingly there were schisms and difficulties – it was often not clear what form Anglicanism would take, when shorn of its missionary roots. When the local churches came of age, the challenges to the European model would be profound. The language of Christianity would be transformed through missionary encounter, so much so that it would begin to reshape the conception of Anglicanism itself.

Sometimes European missionaries died from causes other than illness. Most celebrated was Bishop James Hannington (1847–85) who was consecrated Bishop of Eastern Equatorial Africa in June 1884. He led an expedition that reached Lake Nyanza in 1885, but was murdered on the orders of King Mwanga of Buganda in October 1885. His successor as Bishop of Uganda, Alfred Tucker (1849–1914), was beset with difficulties. There had been conflict between the CMS missionaries and the French Catholic White Fathers. Tucker described the situation in December 1890 as 'like a volcano on the verge of an eruption'. Political events quickly made his situation even more complex – in the end, the CMS had to organize a collection to protect Christians with force. Tucker was impressed by the quality of the emerging Christian elite and, adopting Venn's principles, ordained Africans and ruled that those studying theology should wear the kanzu (long robe). He claimed that he did not want 'to denationalise the Baganda . . . to turn them into black Englishmen (if such a thing were possible) but rather to strengthen their own national characteristics'. In 1897, he sought to develop self-government, although missionaries again feared being subjected to African control.

Africa fights back: missionary conflict

Africanization occurred elsewhere on the continent. While most of the early missions to Africa and India had been the work of Evangelicals, by the middle of the 19th century, the SPG, often supported by the CBF, had been deeply influenced by Tractarianism. After the free churchman David Livingstone published his *Missionary Travels and Researches in South Africa* in 1857, there was a renewed vigour to evangelize Africa, and also to put an end to the slave trade and provide alternative forms of economic activity, particularly in growing cotton. The Universities' Mission to Central Africa was founded in response to Livingstone's appeal in Cambridge when he begged his undergraduate audience to direct their attention to Africa: 'I go back to Africa to make an open path for commerce and Christianity; do you carry out the work which I have begun. I leave it to you.'

The UMCA adopted catholic principles, seeing bishops as pioneers in conversion. The ill-fated Charles Mackenzie, who had been Colenso's Archdeacon, was consecrated in Cape Town by Gray as a 'missionary bishop' in 1860. As Owen Chadwick put it:

> the aim of sending the bishop before the flock was gathered was to plant 'the church in its integrity', to convert not by the distribution of a Bible but by gathering the heathen into a Christian community with a sacramental life.

Mackenzie attempted to penetrate the African interior by sailing up the Zambezi to what is now Malawi. Illness soon took members of the missionary team, including the Bishop in 1862. His successor, William Tozer, withdrew to Zanzibar and adopted a different overland strategy. Working in what became a German colony proved fraught with difficulties, but it also offered a different pattern for evangelization. What developed was an episcopally led process of Africanization. Bishop Smythies who followed him wanted to produce

> a Christian civilisation suited to their own climate and their own circumstances. . . . We do not allow any of our boys in our schools to wear any European clothing; it is not our business to encourage the trade in boots.

The synod of Zanzibar sought to 'strenuously discourage all Europeanisms'. Smythies' successor was Frank Weston, the international leader of the Anglo-Catholics in the 1920s, who continued the policy of Africanization.

Shortly before the First World War, there was controversy between missionary bishops at Kikuyu in East Africa. Following the lead of the Edinburgh Missionary Conference of 1910, which called for reconciliation between missionary societies, three years later the CMS-sponsored Bishops of Mombasa and Uganda invited a Church of Scotland minister to preach and offered communion to free church missionaries. For Weston, this was to deny the importance of the bishop as 'the Christ-given centre of union here on earth'. It was only 'in fellowship with the universal episcopate that East Africa would escape from the peculiarities of Scottish, American, German, and English systems of religious thought, and ultimately assimilate something of the universal religion of the Son of Man.' The 'African Catholic' church was the 'mystic Body of Christ made visible in a certain country amidst a certain people, and therefore exhibiting a local colouring and harmony with its local setting; yet none the less catholic and apostolic'. From his missionary perspective, he sought an African Christianity in part to resist what he regarded as the dilute liberal Christianity of Europe. He wrote to Randall Davidson, Archbishop of Canterbury, that a 'view possible in an Oxford study is not necessarily possible in the mission field. . . . Questions that are left open in academic circles require definite solutions in the world's market-places'. Christianity needed to take its stand by adapting itself to local conditions without diluting its message.

Colenso

In Africa new forms of Anglicanism were being developed. Questions soon emerged about the relations between the churches: who would have the final say when there were disagreements? One of the early appointments of the CBF in 1848 was Robert Gray of Cape Town, whose diocese covered the whole of South Africa. After experiencing considerable hardship trying to visit his diocese (including surviving for six days on a hunk of cheese), he became convinced that it needed dividing for successful missionary work. Natal and Grahamstown were chosen as suitable locations for bishoprics. John W. Colenso (1814–83), author of popular mathematics textbooks, was chosen as Bishop of Natal in 1853. Almost immediately he was embroiled in controversy. He was convinced that God's Spirit extended to everyone, Christian and non-Christian alike. He wrote in his commentary on *Romans* that 'every good thought, which has ever stirred within a heathen's mind, is a token of that work which God's good spirit is working within him'. It was the duty of the missionary to find parallels between Christianity and the native religions. He also held radical views on polygamy, recognizing that all wives needed to be cared for – he did not believe in polygamy but felt it was better than destitution.

Such attitudes, which were compounded by his questioning of much of the literal truth of Old Testament history, led to bitter controversy with Gray. After legal advice, Gray summoned a meeting of bishops to try Colenso, who in the meantime had departed for England. In 1863, Colenso was found guilty in his absence and sentenced to be deposed. There was a long legal process, Colenso refusing to accept Gray's authority as metropolitan (or leading bishop). After the case was heard in London before the Privy Council, Colenso managed to hold on to the endowments of the diocese and remained Bishop of Natal. The argument was that once colonial legislatures were in place the Crown had no rights over bishops, which meant that Gray was not legally metropolitan (despite having been granted letters patent to that effect in 1853 at the cost of £10,000).

After some time, another bishop in communion with Gray was appointed to Natal, adopting the title Bishop of Maritzburg. In England there was confusion about the rights of the two bishops. Convocation said it was in communion with Gray, but refused to excommunicate Colenso. It was clear that something needed to be done to solve the problems of authority: the rights of the English Crown seemed to interfere with the legitimate authority of the independent churches. The South African situation took a long time to settle. Some splinter groups never fully accepted the authority of Cape Town: a Church of England in South Africa still exists, although it owes its modern form to support from the conservative Evangelical diocese of Sydney which led to the appointment of a bishop in 1955.

The effects of the Colenso affair were profound. While not necessarily helpful for Gray and the South African Church, the Colenso ruling was absolutely clear. Where there was self-government, the English Crown had no rights to interfere with the colonial churches. Moreover, four American bishops had been appointed to serve overseas, which would raise the question of parallel jurisdictions. Partly because the role of the Archbishop of Canterbury outside England was not clear, a greater degree of inter-Anglican conversation seemed imperative. Transport links

'The Church's One Foundation'

In 1866, Samuel John Stone, curate of St Paul's, Haggerston, published a hymn collection called *Lyra Fidelium*. It contains just one hymn that is still sung: 'The Church's One Foundation'. There are some particularly direct lines in verse 3:

Though with a scornful wonder
men see her sore opprest,
by schisms rent asunder,
by heresies distrest,
yet saints their watch are keeping,
their cry goes up, 'How long?'
and soon the night of weeping
shall be the morn of song.

This hymn was written, as the author said, 'out of admiration for the opposition shown by Bishop Gray of Cape Town to Bishop Colenso's teaching'.

were becoming faster, and bishops from overseas were invited to conferences, including the 150th anniversary of the SPG in 1851, and to participate in English consecrations. A sense of pan-Anglicanism was developing; the term 'Anglican Communion' began to be used. In 1860, Gray called for a synod of colonial churches, and by 1865 the Canadian bishops formally requested the Archbishop of Canterbury to convene a synod of all the colonial bishops. Gradually it was felt that this should be expanded to include the independent churches of Scotland and America.

The first Lambeth Conference

Archbishop Longley was highly cautious about the first Lambeth Conference, which he summoned in September 1867. Its jurisdiction and power were unclear from the start: even the Archbishop of York refused to attend out of concern for the possible effect on the role of Parliament or Crown over church affairs. Others were anxious about the dominance of High Church colonial bishops. It was clear that it would be a highly circumscribed meeting – there was no hope of establishing a form of spiritual court, or even a definition of what sort of church was represented by the assembled bishops. In the event, 76 bishops attended, meeting without reporters. There was intense lobbying on the matter of Colenso; although 35 bishops signed a letter of support for Gray, the subject was not on the main agenda. At the end of the conference, a declaration was issued containing the various reports that had been received. An encyclical letter was published which was also circulated among leaders of other churches. While there were few concrete outcomes, a new pattern had been adopted: a network of men had gathered from across the globe; the archbishop functioned as a *primus inter pares* and not as an Anglican Pope; matters were debated and discussed, but there was no power to make canons. That it was a collection of bishops without laity was as much a product of the peculiar circumstances of the establishment of the Church of England where lay synodical representation was still a matter of contention. But the effect was that the role of bishops was magnified, which amounted to a victory for the High Churchmen, even if the final resolution called for synods in all places where Anglicanism was not established by law. At the same time, there was little effective central control offered to protect national churches from despotic or heretic bishops: instead, provinces had to do whatever they could to ensure their own checks and balances. History has shown that these have not always been successful.

The Anglican Communion formally established itself in 1867, but its powers were curtailed. By 1874, the final settlement of the Colenso case meant that new metropolitans could be consecrated without taking the oath of obedience: this meant they were free from control, even from the Archbishop of Canterbury. His authority, such as it was, was purely moral. Provincial autonomy – begun in very different circumstances by Henry VIII – remained the central doctrine shaping Anglicanism. The nascent national churches became quite independent of one another. What united them was a doctrinal, liturgical, and historical memory, and (in most churches at least) a sense of Englishness. The course of Anglicanism since this first Lambeth Conference has been a fading of memories, a reshaping of liturgy, and, most importantly, a decolonization of the churches. Meeting every 10 years has served as much to highlight differences as to emphasize similarities.

Chapter 7
The future of Anglicanism

Anglican identity

If Anglicanism had tentatively established itself at the First
Lambeth Conference in 1867 as a global body, it still had little
coherence. Bishop Selwyn, translated to the diocese of Lichfield
shortly afterwards, became the most outspoken champion of the
further development of the Anglican Communion. In a sermon
preached at the Baltimore General Convention of the American
Church in 1871, he outlined the dilemma of Anglicanism: the need
for some form of central authority that was compatible with the
rights of the independent churches. It was 'the duty of all loving
members of the Church to submit their own private opinion, in
matters indifferent, to the judgment of their brethren; . . . There
need be no servile uniformity, if there be but a recognized authority,
which all are willing to obey.' Selwyn sought a central authority to
prevent the excesses which might emerge if national churches
moved too far:

> May we not hope that some central authority, elected and obeyed by
> every member of every branch of the whole Anglican communion,
> may be appointed to exercise this power of controlling inordinate
> self-will, and zeal not tempered with discretion: saying to the too
> hasty minds, who claim as lawful, things which are not expedient,
> 'Thus far shalt thou go, and no further'?

How this was to be done was far from clear: global Anglicanism might need some sort of decision-making body, but it could hardly model itself on the centralized papacy that had been formalized at the First Vatican Council of 1870. Christopher Wordsworth, Bishop of Lincoln, led English opposition to the Vatican decrees, appealing to the unity and equality of all bishops against domination by any one bishop. Anglican churches might claim catholicity, yet how this was to be expressed across the 150 bishops of the Anglican Communion was left unsaid. While a measure of elasticity and adaptability was crucial, there seemed to be a need for some form of inter-provincial authority: a simple meeting of bishops was inadequate to act as an international arbitrator. Selwyn put his case before Convocation in 1873 with the claim (made many years earlier by Archbishop Laud) that the office of the Archbishop should be considered 'equivalent to that of patriarch of the ancient church'. The colonial churches, he maintained, look to the Church of England, for 'a system that would prevent them from diverging so widely from the mother church that we can scarcely recognise them as our own children'. The choice was between independent autonomous national churches with little more than a shared history and culture, and a global confederation of churches with some authority delegated to the Archbishop or his councils.

A second Lambeth Conference was summoned in 1878 with the express aim of working out principles for 'maintaining union among various Churches of the Anglican Communion'. Tait's opening address to the 100 bishops clearly advocated provincial autonomy and toleration of diversity. What emerged was the very opposite of Selwyn's call for a central tribunal. Instead, the Conference recommended that 'the duly certified action of every national or particular Church . . . in the exercise of its own discipline, should be respected by all the other Churches, and by their individual members.' There was to be no meddling in the affairs of other churches and no central tribunal: 'Every ecclesiastical province . . . should be held responsible for its own decisions in the exercise of . . . discipline.' Once again, diversity and elasticity won out against centralism and uniformity. A central council for missionary strategy was proposed and accepted, but never met.

The next Conference of 1888 cemented this arrangement. Convened by the relatively youthful E. W. Benson, it was attended by 145 bishops, among them Samuel Crowther. Various practical issues were discussed, including the thorny issue of polygamy as well as (again) 'mutual relations of dioceses and branches of the Anglican Communion'. Benson's opening address emphasized provincial autonomy: 'the Conference was in no sense a synod and not adapted, or competent, or within its powers, if it should attempt to make binding decisions on doctrines or discipline'. Most of the resolutions were simply suggestions for further study of reports, but some votes were taken. On polygamy, about which Crowther spoke eloquently, Venn's views were maintained: 'Persons living in polygamy' were not to be admitted to baptism, but could be accepted as candidates and kept under Christian instruction until they accepted the law of Christ. However, wives of polygamists could be admitted in some cases to baptism. This was a matter for the local church to decide.

In some places such an approach meant there were very few communicants. In the 1960s, a report from Nigeria suggested that 'probably there is not a single Nigerian in a position of leadership in the denomination who has not been disciplined at some time for marital irregularities'. Given its prevalence in Africa, polygamy continued to feature on Lambeth agendas through the 20th century. It was only in 1988 that Colenso's views were finally adopted: while upholding monogamy as the ideal, the Conference recommended 'that a polygamist who responds to the Gospel and wishes to join the Anglican Church may be baptized and confirmed with his believing wives and children' provided that he promised not to marry again. The polygamist 'shall not be compelled to put away any of his wives, on account of the social deprivation they would suffer'. A compromise solution was made to an issue of sexuality. Later in the 20th century, another sexual issue, that of homosexuality, proved less acceptable to many than polygamy.

Archbishop Benson was concerned to safeguard the autonomy of the different churches. His hero was Cyprian, the defender of the equality of bishops, about whom he published a book shortly before he died. Before his translation to Canterbury, Benson had been first bishop of Truro, where he shaped a vision of the church that drew on the historical Celtic and independent heritage of Cornwall. He continued to promote such 'contextual' theology at Canterbury:

> It is for the Anglican communion in the power of its own unity to rear on the earth colonial churches, native churches, national churches (in some instances embracing many races) like herself, yet different – churches which shall weave for Christ the local life, the natural genius, the hereditary sentiment, into the framework and setting of ritual, hymn, or article, as they have interwoven in our own nation-church.

Whatever it meant for the Anglican Communion, it did not imply a monolithic unity imposed from above. For Benson, 'Unity is not the first scene, but the last triumph of Christianity and man. Christ himself could not *create* unity in His Church. He could pray for it, and his prayer most movingly teaches us to work for it. On earth it is not a gift, but a growth.' Like Selwyn, Benson used the term 'elasticity' which could allow for different solutions in different places. Commenting on the Japanese Mission, Benson noted that 'the great end of our planting a Church in Japan is that there may be a Japanese Church, not an English Church'. Benson remained loyal to the principles of national churches against a monolithic Anglicanism.

The Chicago–Lambeth Quadrilateral

The most important aspect of the 1888 Conference was its consideration of what became known as the 'Chicago–Lambeth Quadrilateral' adopted unanimously as Resolution 11. It was based upon one that had been earlier submitted to the 1886 Chicago General Convention of the American Church. It was principally the work of William Reed Huntington, one of the most influential American churchmen of his time and the greatest single voice in the revision of the Prayer Book. In his 1870 work, *The Church-Idea*, he sought the 'absolutely essential features of the Anglican position' as a way of establishing wider unity between the churches after the Civil War. Against the view that Anglicanism was little more than a vague feeling of Englishness, he sought for the pared-down fundamentals that he regarded as the 'Anglican principle':

The Chicago–Lambeth Quadrilateral (1888)

1. The Holy Scriptures of the Old and New Testaments, as 'containing all things necessary to salvation', and as being the rule and ultimate standard of faith.
2. The Apostles' Creed, as the baptismal symbol; and the Nicene Creed, as the sufficient statement of the Christian faith.
3. The two sacraments ordained by Christ himself – Baptism and the Supper of the Lord – ministered with unfailing use of Christ's words of institution, and of the elements ordained by him.
4. The historic episcopate, locally adapted in the methods of its administration, to the varying needs of the nations and peoples called of God into the unity of his Church.

Because the English State-Church has muffled these first principles in a cloud of non-essentials . . . she mourns today the loss of half her children. Only by avoiding the like fatal error can the American branch of the Anglican Church hope to save herself from becoming in effect, whatever she may be in name, a sect. Only by a wise discrimination between what can and what cannot be conceded for the sake of unity, is unity attainable.

Church unity required the four simple points of the quadrilateral and no more. There was no mention of England, Anglicanism, the Reformation, the Thirty-Nine Articles, or the Book of Common Prayer. Although Huntington argued for the episcopate on the basis of a reasonable claim to general acceptance, the Chicago Convention spiced it up with the word 'historic'. Bishops thereby became 'incapable of compromise or surrender' and 'essential to the restoration of unity'. Whereas both Huntington and the American bishops were concerned with the reunion of the American Church after the Civil War, the international context of the Anglican Communion meant that the Lambeth version was more far-reaching. In the desire for clarity, episcopacy was elevated into the essence of the Church: churches with other forms of oversight could not be embraced by Anglicans as true churches unless they accepted the historic episcopate (by which most meant apostolic succession, even if they did not explicitly say so).

This insistence might have come as a surprise to many earlier Anglican authors. Even in 1888, there were alternative views on offer. Following others who saw church order as an 'indifferent' matter, J. B. Lightfoot, Bishop of Durham, claimed that church orders were 'aids and expedients' which 'a Christian could not afford to hold lightly or to neglect. But they were no part of the *essence* of God's message to man in the Gospel.' Similarly, F. D. Maurice, whose understanding of the church resembles the Lambeth Quadrilateral, did not regard bishops as essential for the church. During the debates over the Anglo-Prussian Jerusalem Bishopric, he wrote: 'Shall I require the German, or the Helvetian, or the

Dutchman to say, I have had no church, not even the dream of one, I come to ask one from you? God forbid.'

The unequivocal insistence on bishops at Lambeth 1888 universalized one particular aspect of the 1662 Act of Uniformity across a communion where relations with non-episcopal churches were often of vital missionary importance. Historically, the Church of England had insisted on episcopacy within its own domains but had not sought to impose it on those who had lost it for one reason or another. As Archbishop William Wake (1657–1737) wrote to a French Catholic priest, who had been concerned that Archbishop Grindal had granted a licence to a presbyterian minister: 'I should be unwilling to affirm that where the ministry is not episcopal, there is no church, nor any true administration of the sacraments.' After 1888, such elasticity over ministry was no longer possible: this would prove deeply divisive through the 20th century.

Anglicanism into the 20th century

The pattern had been set for future Lambeth Conferences: in 1897 there was further discussion about the idea of an Anglican tribunal. This was resisted, largely through the opposition of the American bishops with their long experience of ecclesiastical and political independence. Provincial autonomy was also emphasized by the title of Archbishop being conferred on the Metropolitans of Sydney, Cape Town, and Jamaica. Anglicanism was not going to be a pale imitation of Rome, but something quite different. By 1908, the numbers of bishops invited to Lambeth had increased to 242, partly because of the revival of Suffragan (assistant) bishops in English dioceses. There were still only two black bishops, both from West Africa.

The Conference was preceded by an international gathering, which for the first time included laity and clergy as well as bishops from across the Communion. This pan-Anglican Congress was the brainchild of Bishop H. H. Montgomery (1847–1932), secretary of the SPG, which he saw as the 'foreign office' for world Anglicanism. The Congress, which attracted up to 17,000 people daily, served to foster a more tangible sense of communion, but it carried no decision-making authority. The Conference itself was deeply aware of the breadth of the Communion: while resolutions on moral issues (including contraception and divorce) were conservative, there was increasing recognition of cultural diversity, which began to lead to Prayer Book revision. In somewhat patronizing language, the bishops saw the need to depart from the historic liturgies: 'every effort should be made, under due authority, to render the forms of public worship more intelligible to uneducated congregations and better suited to the widely diverse needs of the various races within the Anglican Communion'.

Indigenous leadership

Equally important at the 1908 Lambeth Conference was the stress it placed on one bishop for all people in one place: 'All races and peoples, whatever their language or conditions, must be welded into one Body.' The model drawn was purely geographical. Yet in a period when almost all bishops were European or North American, this could be seen as stultifying the development of a 'native' leadership. Despite the next resolution, which urged the importance of 'a native episcopate in all countries where the Church is planted', it was not until the breakdown of the colonial system after the Second World War that significant numbers of indigenous leaders emerged.

A white leadership, however, could prove deeply troublesome to the state. This was demonstrated by the stand taken by much of the white South African leadership against the institutionalization of Apartheid in the 1960s. A historically quiescent episcopate was radicalized: 'if the Bill [to introduce the pass laws] were to become law', they commented, 'we should ourselves be unable to obey it or counsel our clergy and people to do so'. Geoffrey Clayton, Archbishop of Cape Town, saw the need for a multi-racial church with a non-European leadership, which would 'not always be content to deliver the message in an English dress'. Working against injustice became increasingly important, leading to the witness of Trevor Huddleston, a friend of the future leaders of the ANC, and eventually Desmond Tutu, the first black Archbishop of Cape Town, whose leadership assisted in the peaceful transition to a multi-racial state.

The perceived cultural imperialism of a white church leadership exercising authority over marginalized people led the Church of New Zealand from the 1970s to question the policy of assimilation of the indigenous Maori population. In 1978, the Maori 'Te Pihopatanga o Aotearoa' was inaugurated as a semi-autonomous body with representation in the General Synod. This was followed in 1992 by a revised Constitution (which also included Polynesia) which sought to create equality in decision-making. While the New Zealand dioceses remained unchanged, regional bishoprics were set up within 'Te Pihopatanga o Aotearoa'.

The Church of England

During the 20th century, the Church of England became increasingly like the churches it had planted: there was a widespread desire for independence from political control. Calls for a form of synodical government led to the Life and Liberty Movement under the leadership of William Temple, which culminated in the Enabling Act of 1919, which gave the Church of England some degree of autonomy through a Church Assembly. Local churches were also given a measure of lay control through Parochial Church Councils. Nevertheless, measures had to be presented to a Parliament which was still prepared to flex its muscle, as with its rejection of the proposed 1928 Prayer Book. It took until 1974 before the Church of England, which had reformed its structures in 1970 with a General Synod and lower synods, was finally given the authority to reform its liturgy. Only in 1976 was the Church given the major say in appointing senior clergy, although even now Prime Ministers are able to reject names presented to them. The Church of England may resemble other provinces, but the power of Establishment still runs deep.

The 20th century was also marked by a number of theological controversies in the Church of England, which sometimes had international repercussions. Frank Weston of Zanzibar, for instance, made frequent broadsides against modernism and liberalism. He was anxious that the attempt of many of his erstwhile Oxford tutors to make Christianity acceptable to the 'cultivated modern man', would water down the claims of the Gospel. B. H. Streeter, for instance, edited the notorious collection *Foundations* in 1912, in which he denied the bodily resurrection of Christ. When Streeter was appointed canon of Hereford cathedral in 1915, Weston excommunicated the bishop. Others, like Hensley Henson, who became Bishop of Durham, were denounced for questioning the virgin birth. The Modern Churchmen's Union was established to promote critical theological thought through a journal and often controversial conferences. Apparent denials of the divinity of Christ at Cambridge in 1921 led the archbishops to set up a doctrine commission under Temple. Their long-awaited report of 1938 revealed the huge variety of opinion in the Church of England and lack of unanimity.

Through the century, doctrinal controversies have been repeated at various intervals. Most important was the publication of *Honest to God* in 1963 by John Robinson, Bishop of Woolwich. This little book popularized many radical theological ideas, calling for an end to what Robinson regarded as outmoded superstition and myth. A newspaper quoted him as saying 'Our image of God must go'. At a time when the church was under threat from increasing secularization and a serious decline in clergy numbers and churchgoers, theology was for the first time being debated in the mass media. However, sensationalism and over-reaction meant that the opportunity for serious theological discussion was soon lost: efforts to correlate Christian faith to modern thought were derided

Prayer Book revision

After the first tentative efforts in Ireland and the United States, Prayer Book revision quickly became a concern of most provinces. The balance between cultural relevance and theological issues proved complex. The fact that partisan identity was frequently expressed through liturgical practice compounded the issue and often led to heated debate, usually overcome through a variety of options. In England the rejection of the 1928 Prayer Book led to widespread use of unauthorized liturgies and calls for disestablishment. Later, many liturgical scholars criticized the Book of Common Prayer on historical grounds in the desire to achieve a more 'primitive' version of the liturgy. By the 1958 Lambeth Conference, it was acknowledged that the Prayer Book was no longer the basis for unity. In many places there is now virtually no historical memory of the formulas of the traditional Books of Common Prayer in their English or American versions. New liturgies respond to very different cultures. What Cranmer would have made of the following prayer is hard to imagine:

The Book of Common Prayer 1979 (ECUSA) (Eucharistic Prayer C)

God of all power, Ruler of the Universe, you are worthy of glory and praise.
Glory to you for ever and ever.
At your command all things came to be: the vast expanse of interstellar space, galaxies, suns, the planets in their courses, and this fragile earth, our island home.

> *By your will they were created and have their being.*
>
> **From primal elements you brought forth the human race, and blessed us with memory, reason, and skill. You made us the rulers of creation. But we turned against you, and betrayed your trust; and we turned against one another.**
>
> *Have mercy, Lord, for we are sinners in your sight.*

as 'South Bank Theology', or dismissed, in the words of the Evangelical leader J. I. Packer, as half-digested German liberal theology: a 'plateful of mashed-up Tillich, fried in Bultmann and garnished with Bonhoeffer'.

The Church of England returned instead to debating its liturgies, working out how to close down churches, and to new evangelistic crusades (like Donald Coggan's moralistic 'Call to the Nation' in the 1970s). The few efforts to engage with youth culture by men like David Collyer, 'chaplain to the unattached', relied on strong personality, and could not be institutionalized. In the 40 years from 1960, membership of the Church of England has halved: in 1960 there were 190,713 confirmations; this had fallen to 97,620 in 1980, and a mere 40,881 in 1997.

Nevertheless, the Church of England maintained a strong political and national presence through much of the century. Most importantly, William Temple, Archbishop of Canterbury from 1942, was the architect of the welfare state, and an inspirational leader across the theological and political divide. Others, like George Bell, Bishop of Chichester, spoke out against what they perceived as the excesses of Allied bombing during the Second World War. Temple's successor, Geoffrey Fisher, failed to capitalize on his predecessor's example, but something lived on in the influential report *Faith in the City* of 1984, which called for serious engagement by the church in the alleviation of social problems. During the 1980s, at a time of weak parliamentary opposition, Church of England leaders took on an increasingly political role.

The 1990s saw efforts to make the archbishops into executive directors working through a board (the Archbishops' Council), which has failed to do anything to halt decline. Such managerialism sits uneasily with synodical and episcopal government. Whether the Church of England can any longer call on the passive support of a sympathetic majority in the multicultural society of contemporary Britain is an open question. Its inheritance as a national church, which carried it through the inter-war period as far as the 1980s, can no longer be taken for granted. As a recent writer on William Temple has put it: 'The belief that society could, or should, pursue a single, broadly agreed version of virtue, or the good life, was abandoned' from the 1960s onwards. The church ceased to be the major voice in the state after the idea of a 'national character' on which that state was built collapsed. It is hardly surprising that it has become embroiled in inward-looking controversies over sexual morality. In its current state, the Church of England is a microcosm of the Anglican Communion – the same tensions threaten to divide it. Its relative weakness and rapid decline mean that it can no longer take for granted its position as the mother church of Anglicanism.

Ecumenism

The Lambeth Conference of 1920 was delayed because of the First World War. One of its main concerns was the visible unity of all Christians, a move which resembled the secular efforts at international co-operation in the League of Nations. Resolution 9 was drafted by Bishop Palmer of Bombay and V. S. Azariah of Dorkal, the first Indian bishop. It deplored division and called for a visible fellowship between episcopal and non-episcopal churches of all 'who profess and call themselves Christians'. While the four principles of the Lambeth Quadrilateral of 1888 were restated, teaching on the ministry was modified. Other forms of ministry 'have been manifestly blessed and owned by the Holy Spirit as effective means of grace'. Although the removal of the phrase 'historic episcopate' was bound to annoy some Anglo-Catholics, the resolution commanded widespread support. Nevertheless, the Lambeth bishops repeated the claim that episcopacy 'is now and will prove to be in the future the best instrument for maintaining the unity and continuity of the Church'. The intention was that ministers who had not received episcopal ordination would receive it. Although their earlier ministries were not to be regarded as deficient, they were nevertheless asked to make a sacrifice for the 'sake of a common fellowship, a common ministry, and a common service to the world'.

The Lambeth Appeal became a landmark in the nascent ecumenical movement. Discussions soon began with the Orthodox churches as well as the small European Old Catholic Churches (which had separated from Rome). Both were invited to send observers to the 1930 Lambeth Conference, when hope was expressed for the 'ultimate reunion of all Christendom'. The Old Catholics were received into full communion in 1931. Close ties developed with the Church of Sweden, which had retained the historic episcopate. This finally led to intercommunion with most of the Nordic and British churches in the Porvoo Agreement of 1993.

The Appeal gave licence to the South Indian Reunion scheme. By 1930, the four southern dioceses of Madras, Travancore, Cochin, and Dornakal were permitted to enter into negotiations. At the Lambeth Conference of that year the scheme came under discussion: some Anglo-Catholics, including the Bishop of Colombo, were outspoken opponents. In the end, however, the resolutions, brought forward by William Temple, passed with hardly any dissent. The scheme made progress in the 1930s and the union of four denominations (Anglican, Presbyterian, Congregationalist, and Methodist) was formally inaugurated on the day that India became independent in 1947.

After the Second World War, the Lambeth Conferences resumed in 1948: the South Indian bishops were not invited, having put themselves out of communion for the sake of ecumenism. They returned to the fold only when all had received episcopal ordination. Some felt that churches elsewhere might follow the Indian lead. In 1946, Geoffrey Fisher, Archbishop of Canterbury, suggested to members of the British Free Churches that they might take episcopacy into their own system. Denominations would disappear for the greater good, provided that what emerged would be 'a Church with which the Anglican Churches could eventually be in full communion'.

Comprehensiveness

At the 1948 Conference, a group of bishops noted that there was something important about Anglicanism, with its odd blend of parties and dispersed authority, that might serve the wider church:

> We believe it is only through a comprehensiveness which makes it possible to hold together in the Anglican Communion understandings of truth which are held in separation in other churches, that the Anglican Communion is able to reach out in different directions and so to fulfil its special vocation as one of God's instruments for the restoration of the visible unity of his whole church.

The Anglican Communion, they held, had a 'dispersed rather than a centralised authority'. It had many elements which contributed to 'a process of mutual support, mutual checking, and redressing of errors or exaggerations in the many-sided fullness of the authority which Christ has committed to His Church'. While such diversity was never formally adopted by the Conference, it displayed a desire for an open and continued conversation, reminiscent of William Temple's introduction to the Church of England's Doctrine Commission Report of 1938:

Our aim is ... to promote unity and mutual appreciation in the Church of England, partly by the interpretation of one school of thought, and partly by pointing to the fulness of a truth diversely apprehended in different quarters.

Some commentators have seen comprehensiveness as a recipe for anarchy. Stephen Sykes, one of the leading writers on Anglicanism, regards it as an 'open invitation to intellectual laziness and self-deception' and a 'failure to be frank about the issues between the parties in the Church of England'. While such criticisms contain an element of truth, the method of comprehensiveness also suggests something else: parties, at least when they are open to one another, each pursue a truth which none fully possesses. The 1968 Lambeth Conference Report noted that comprehensiveness

implies that the apprehension of truth is a growing thing: we only gradually succeed in 'knowing the truth' ... Comprehensiveness implies a willingness to allow liberty of interpretation, with a certain slowness in arresting or resisting exploratory thinking.

Truth was a clamour rather than a possession.

Similarly, Michael Ramsey, Archbishop of Canterbury through the 1960s, held that Anglican theology was no 'confessionalism', but the 'catholic method' itself. All churches, he said in *The Gospel and the Catholic Church*, point beyond themselves to

the Gospel of God by which alone, in which alone, in one universal family, mankind can be made perfect. It is not something Roman or Greek or Anglican; rather does it declare to men their utter dependence upon Christ by setting forth the universal Church in which all that is Anglican or Roman or Greek or partial or local in any way must share in an agonizing death to its pride.

For Ramsey, the Christian was asked to participate in the death and resurrection of Christ. This delivered him or her 'from partial rationalisms' into an 'orthodoxy which no individual and no group can possess'. Ramsey summarized this tersely: 'Hither alone the church shall point; and here men shall know the Truth and the Truth shall make them free.'

The Anglican Consultative Council

This emphasis on searching for the truth meant that there would inevitably be diversity. Yet what were to be the limits of this diversity? If Anglicanism was simply a group of national churches loosely united by a degree of shared history, then how was coherence to be achieved? There still seemed to be the need for some inter-Anglican body. By Lambeth 1958, there was a call for an executive officer to relieve some of the burden from the Archbishop of Canterbury, and to oversee the work of the Anglican Council on Missionary Strategy and the Consultative Body of the Lambeth Conference. The first postholder was Stephen Bayne, Episcopal Bishop of Olympia, who possessed 'the gift of bestowing on others the gift he had in conversation'. In 1963, at the Toronto Anglican Congress, a scheme for Moral Responsibility and Interdependence was initiated as an attempt to share knowledge and resources between rich and poor provinces. By 1968, it seemed imperative to establish an institution (one of the so-called 'Instruments of Unity') which could meet more frequently (and economically) than the Lambeth Conference, and which would also represent synodical government more transparently.

The Anglican Consultative Council was established to share information, to advise on 'inter-Anglican, provincial, and diocesan relationships, including the division of provinces'; to develop agreed mission policies and to share resources; to ensure collaboration with other churches; to advise on proposals for future union negotiations; and 'to advise on problems in inter-Anglican communication and to help in the dissemination of Anglican and ecumenical information'. It has met as a forum for discussion about every two years, with a membership of a bishop, priest, and layperson from larger provinces, together with two from the smaller provinces (a bishop and priest or layperson). The Council has kept to its brief: its status and authority remain unclear.

Primates' Meeting

A further move towards inter-provincial communication has been the (so-called) Primates' Meeting, which was established in 1978 by Archbishop Donald Coggan as an opportunity for 'leisurely thought, prayer and deep consultation'. This group, which comprises primates (which had replaced the term 'metropolitan') and presiding bishops under the chair of the Archbishop of Canterbury, has frequently been the scene of heated debate. Primates were limited to one per national church whatever its size. This meant two of the four oldest primates of the Anglican Communion (York and Dublin) were not included. More importantly, very small churches (like those of Scotland) had the same representation as massive churches like those of Nigeria. Again, there is a lack of coherence and an absence of synodical accountability: the meeting has refused to acknowledge anything more than a consultative and advisory authority.

Given this lack of clarity, the Inter-Anglican Doctrinal and Theological Commission was set up to consider proposals from the Lambeth Conference of 1988 to clarify the nature of Communion and the Instruments of Unity, especially the recommendation that the primates should develop a 'collegial role'. The Virginia Report of 1996 raised many questions about the function of the instruments of unity:

> Should primates be expected to make authoritative statements, or should the primates' meeting be encouraged to exercise a primarily pastoral role? . . . What is the relationship of the Primates' Meeting to the Lambeth Conference and the ACC?

While it was suggested that a larger bureaucracy might ensure better communication, it was still not clear where authority rested. Tensions were being stretched to breaking point.

Whereas on polygamy and women priests the Instruments of Unity were able to respond to unilateral action so that churches could agree to live with different practices without breaking communion, even if there were degrees of impairment, the reaction to the consecration of a homosexual bishop has been quite different. It brings to a head major differences over Biblical interpretation and the authority of Scripture, but it also displays the global re-alignment of the Communion in the post-colonial world. The historic mother churches of the old colonizers are no longer the geographical or spiritual centre of the communion. Africa and Asia are flexing their muscles against Europe and North America with their liberal ways.

Women and ministry

By the end of the 19th century, women had begun to play a part in the ministry of some of the churches in the Anglican Communion. In the Church of England deaconesses were appointed from 1862, 'set apart' by the laying on of hands. They were modelled on the German example, primarily to carry out 'diaconal' work including nursing and teaching rather than the ministry of word and sacrament. The 1889 General Convention of the US Episcopal Church authorized deaconesses. For a long time there was ambiguity at the Lambeth Conferences about whether deaconesses were in 'holy orders': Lambeth 1920 resolved that they were; ten years later this was withdrawn.

In June 1943, Bishop R. O. Hall of Hong Kong wrote to William Temple, Archbishop of Canterbury, to say that in the emergency situation caused by the Japanese occupation, he had given permission to Deaconess Florence Lei Tim-Oi (Figure 14) to celebrate communion.

14. Florence Lei Tim-Oi, first woman priest of the Anglican Communion at a 1987 service on her 80th birthday

The following January he ordained her priest, writing to Temple: 'I have had an amazing feeling of quiet conviction about this – as if it was how God wanted it to happen rather than a formal regularisation first.' Although Temple did not have any theoretical objection to the ordination of women, he condemned the action as 'contrary to the laws and precedents of the church'. Despite being given unanimous approval by her diocesan synod, Tim-Oi surrendered her licence after the war without resigning her orders. Lambeth 1948 declined to allow other deaconesses to be ordained priest. Nevertheless, the precedent had been set: it was possible for provinces to ordain women unilaterally.

In response to the huge changes in the recognition of the gifts of women through the 1960s, the 1968 Lambeth Conference asked churches to consider the ordination of women and to report back to the first meeting of the ACC in 1973, which resolved that if any bishop 'acting with the approval of his Province' decided to ordain women to the priesthood, it would be acceptable to the Council, which would 'use its good offices to encourage all Provinces of the Anglican Communion to continue in communion with these dioceses'. Although the decision (which was restated at Lambeth 1978) was only narrowly carried, it meant churches could proceed with the ordination of women. The principle of provincial autonomy was asserted to justify the diversity of practice across the communion.

In the late 1960s, the US Episcopal Women's Caucus began calling for women's ordination, and in 1970 the General Convention voted to allow women to proceed to the diaconate. Three years later there were 97 women deacons. In July 1974 11 women were ordained 'irregularly' in Philadelphia by two retired and one resigned bishop. This action was denounced by the House of Bishops, and attempts were made to prevent the women from exercising priestly ministry. When a Washington rector invited a woman priest to celebrate communion in his church later in the year, he was charged with violating canon law. Similar acts of defiance continued until the 1976 General Convention voted that 'no one shall be denied access' to ordination as deacon, priest, or bishop on the basis of their sex. The irregularly ordained priests were 'regularized', and by the end of the year there were about 100 women priests. Some bishops refused to ordain women, although by 2004 there were only three dioceses where women's ordination was not recognized.

Other provinces followed suit, so that by the late 1990s about half had proceeded with women's ordination: the Church of England voted to allow women priests in 1992. A few hundred clergy resigned from their posts and were offered financial compensation. Provision was made for parishes to vote not to accept their ministry, and in a theologically bizarre piece of legislation allowed them to petition for pastoral care from a bishop who did not ordain women. This principle of 'extended episcopal oversight' has set a precedent that might have far-reaching implications in settling the disputes over the ordination of practising homosexuals.

A number of provinces moved ahead with the consecration of women as bishops. The 1985 ECUSA General Convention expressed its intention 'not to withhold consent to the election of a bishop on the grounds of gender'. The importance of 'listening' to those of different opinions was stressed, and in 1988 the Lambeth Conference resolved that 'each province respect the decision and attitudes of other provinces in the ordination or consecration of women to the episcopate, without such respect necessarily indicating acceptance of the principles involved, maintaining the highest possible degree of communion with the provinces which differ'. The division in the Communion over the ordination of women was made all the more obvious when bishops would no longer be recognized across the communion.

A number of women priests were ordained bishop, including Barbara Harris, suffragan Bishop of Massachusetts, and Penny Jameson, diocesan Bishop of Dunedin in New Zealand. Eleven women bishops attended the 1998 Lambeth Conference. While there have been tensions between provinces, there has been a general willingness to listen and to accommodate diversity. Provincial autonomy has been accepted, even though there is an inevitable untidiness. While the consecration of women as bishops was evidently a novelty, there was no obvious threat to widely accepted patterns of morality: allowing women in leadership roles might challenge the established hierarchies of the church and relationships between the sexes, but it could hardly be said to be countenancing immorality. The same proved not to be case for homosexuality.

Homosexuality

The 1976 ECUSA General Convention affirmed that 'homosexual persons are children of God who have a full and equal claim with all other persons upon the love, acceptance, and pastoral concern and care of the Church'. It resolved to set up a study group to consider the ordination of homosexuals. This had been provoked in part by an American campaigning group ('Integrity'), one of whose vice-presidents, Ellen Barrett, was ordained priest in 1977. Discussions continued through the 1980s and 1990s, with a gradual acceptance of sexual relations outside marriage. Nevertheless, no firm conclusions were reached about either the ordination of practising homosexuals or the blessing of same-sex unions.

The issue of sexuality provoked a showdown at the Lambeth Conference of 1998 (Figure 15). A briefing paper called for a postponement of the vote on homosexuality and for further dialogue so that some workable consensus could be reached, as had happened over women bishops. At the last minute, however, things changed. Nine bishops, mainly from the global South, issued a letter calling on bishops to suspend 'both the ordination of practising homosexuals and the blessing of same sex relationships'. The crucial issue, they held, was 'whether we are in danger of allowing [modern, globalizing] culture with its philosophical assumptions, economic system, sexual alternatives, and hidden idols to determine what we become'. The debate was attended by about 200 bishops and dealt with other pressing moral questions as well as human sexuality. The draft report was modest in its aims, recognizing that the bishops were 'not of one mind about homosexuality'. It simply confirmed the past Conference's statement that sexuality is 'intended by God to find its rightful and full expression between one man and one woman in the covenant of marriage'. While much of the draft report found its way into the final resolution, the debate, chaired by the Archbishop of Armagh, Robin Eames, overran. A number of aggressively worded resolutions were discussed. One

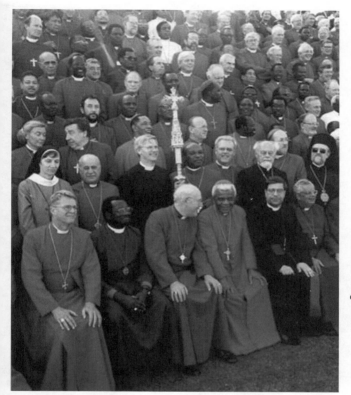

15. The worldwide faith: bishops at the 1998 Lambeth Conference

such declared that to allow homosexual ordination would be 'to commit evangelical suicide'.

What emerged was a major divide between conservatives and liberals. The global shift in Anglicanism was asserting itself. The post-colonial fight-back, with support from Western conservatives, meant that the final Lambeth resolution was toughened with the insertion of a brief text declaring that 'homosexual practice is incompatible with Scripture'. It was accepted by 526 to 70, with 45 abstentions. While the exhortations of the original draft to listen to homosexual persons, to reject homophobia and to monitor developments were accepted, all homosexual activity was ruled out by the short clause: if homosexuality was unscriptural then further dialogue was pointless. Over 100 bishops issued a 'Pastoral Statement to Lesbian and Gay Anglicans,' expressing their 'continued respect and support' and desire to listen. Hardly surprisingly, many dioceses in North America were outraged by the procedure and what appeared as a hijacking of the debate. In other places the resolution was elevated into a bastion of orthodoxy. The Lambeth Conference was being transformed from a forum of conversation with little decision-making authority into something approaching a council of the church. The battle lines were being drawn.

ECUSA was forced to continue its own dialogue but in a quite different spirit. There was a call at the 2000 General Convention to ensure that 'safe spaces' were created to listen to homosexuals. Provocatively, in 2003 the Diocese of New Hampshire elected Gene Robinson, a divorcee in a same-sex relationship, as Bishop (Figure 16). Reactions were predictable. The American Anglican Council, a conservative lobby group, thought it showed 'how far much of the Episcopal Church has moved out of the thriving mainstream of worldwide Anglicanism'. Others were more content: Bishop Chilton Knudsen of Maine remarked (apparently without irony): 'Reconciliation happens when Gene is present; the movement of grace is apparent in every dimension of his ministry.'

Shortly afterwards, the General Convention met in Minneapolis where the bishops confirmed Robinson's election on a vote of 62 for and 43 against. Each diocese, they claimed, had the right to appoint its own bishop, and while 'sexual discipline and holiness of life must be a very serious consideration', they affirmed 'the responsibility of dioceses to discern and raise up fit persons for the ministry of word and sacrament'. The long history of American ecclesiastical independence meant that unilateral action had become a diocesan,

16. Bishop Gene Robinson, the first openly homosexual bishop in the Anglican Communion, receiving his Mitre from his partner

rather than a provincial or international matter: the impact on the global communion was not considered crucial compared with the right of the diocese to act alone. The old political doctrine of 'states' rights' had won against 'federal' Anglicanism.

This confirmation brought to a head the divisions in the American Church, especially since the General Convention had also ruled that 'local faith communities' could 'explore and experience liturgies celebrating and blessing same-sex unions', a move replicated in the Canadian Diocese of New Westminster. Discussion had become increasingly polarized. Dissenting American bishops looked to the Primates 'to intervene in the pastoral emergency that has overtaken us'. In England, the nomination of Jeffrey John, a celibate homosexual, as a suffragan bishop in the diocese of Oxford, provoked a huge outcry, and he was eventually forced to step down. The new Archbishop of Canterbury, Rowan Williams, the leading British theologian, was immediately faced with a crisis. He expressed his hope that the Episcopal Church and the rest of the Communion would have a chance to reflect more deeply on such actions 'before significant and irrevocable decisions are made in response'. Since some provinces were threatening excommunication, there was an urgent need to make the Instruments of Unity work.

In October 2003, the Primates met at Lambeth. Re-affirming the 1998 resolutions, they saw the need to listen to homosexuals and to one another, but also noted that

> the Diocese of New Westminster and the Episcopal Church (USA) ... appear to a number of provinces to have [altered] unilaterally the teaching of the Anglican Communion on this issue. ... Whilst we recognise the juridical autonomy of each province in our Communion, the mutual interdependence of the provinces means that none has authority unilaterally to substitute an alternative teaching as if it were the teaching of the entire Anglican Communion.

To some, it seemed as if action across provincial boundaries was justified: there was a need for 'adequate provision for episcopal oversight of dissenting minorities'. Several African and Asian bishops had already made connections with dissenting American parishes: it looked likely that such inter-provincial practices would continue. For instance, Moses Tay, Bishop of Singapore, had such anxieties about the unorthodoxy of some provinces that he was prepared to appoint bishops to cross boundaries.

A Commission was set up under Robin Eames which produced the Windsor Report in October 2004. It discussed the principle of unilateral action in the framework of different ways of interpreting Scripture. The main problem was the absence of authority in the Communion and the lack of canon law. The Report called for 'Communion-wide dimensions of theological discourse' and suggested a framework for inter-provincial consultation which would be adopted into the canon law of the different provinces: only then would unilateral action be constrained by other considerations.

Into the future

For the Anglican Communion to hold together, there will need to be a strengthening of inter-Anglican bodies, as the Windsor Report suggests. However, whether provinces who regard their actions as right will be prepared to exercise the necessary restraint to allow such bodies to work is an open question. Provincial autonomy may be too firmly entrenched. In 2005, the Primates recognized 'the sensitive balance between provincial autonomy and the expression of critical opinion by others on the internal actions of a Province'. The future of the Communion rests with how this relationship is settled. History reveals that there can be no compulsion: attempts to make authoritative decisions (as at Lambeth 1998) do little more than polarize an already divided church. While reaffirming the Lambeth Resolution, the 2005 ACC nevertheless set in motion the 'listening process'. Whether this is possible is an open question. Indeed, cultural differences might be so extreme that conversation will prove impossible and different provinces will go it alone.

These present disputes point to several different futures for the Communion. First, it is possible that there will be a global realignment of Christians in which pan-Evangelicalism or new progressive alignments will be far more important than Anglicanism. Second, it may be that there will be a far vaguer Anglican body loosely united around a shared history but not necessarily in communion with the see of Canterbury – with the setting up of several global networks (e.g. the Anglican Communion Network) this is certainly feasible. There will be much cross-provincial activity to provide for dissenting congregations. But there is a third possibility that might just keep the Communion together: diversity and comprehensiveness might be at the heart of an Anglicanism that understands itself more as a way of muddling through to the truth than a set of definitive judgements. The desire to listen and to enter into conversation requires voluntary restraint and self-denial among the different factions. The problem is that in a world which seeks clear decisions and absolute certainties such Christian humility might not any longer be considered a virtue.

References and further reading

Sources

The *Parker Society* volumes published by Cambridge University Press
contain a huge number of writings of the English and continental
reformers as well as puritans (for example, Cranmer, Jewel, Grindal,
and Whitgift).

The *Library of Anglo-Catholic Theology* (Oxford: Parker) contains a
wide range of 'high church' theology, mainly from the 17th century,
including Laud and Andrewes.

There are many editions of Richard Hooker's works; the most popular is
John Keble's Oxford University Press edition of 1862. The standard
modern critical edition is the Folger edition published by Harvard
University Press.

Roger Coleman (ed.), *Resolutions of the Twelve Lambeth Conferences*
(Toronto: Anglican Book Centre, 1992).

Resolutions of the Lambeth Conferences are now posted on the Web at
http://www.anglicancommunion.org/acns/archive/index.html

There are a large number of Anglo-Catholic and other resources posted
at 'Project Canterbury': *http://anglicanhistory.org/*

P. E. More and F. L. Cross, *Anglicanism* (London: SPCK, 1935) contains a selection of 17th-century texts.

Geoffrey Rowell, Kenneth Stevenson, and Rowan Williams (eds.), *Love's Redeeming Work: The Anglican Quest for Holiness* (Oxford: Oxford University Press, 2001).

G. R. Evans and J. Robert Wright, *The Anglican Tradition: A Handbook of Sources* (London: SPCK, 1991).

James M. Rosenthal and Nicola Currie (eds.), *Being Anglican in the Third Millennium* (Harrisburg, PA: Morehouse, 1997).

General

Paul Avis, *The Anglican Understanding of the Church: An Introduction* (London: SPCK, 2000).

K. Hylson-Smith, *The Churches in England from Elizabeth I to Elizabeth II*, 2 vols (London: SCM, 1996).

Alister McGrath, *The SPCK Handbook of Anglican Theologians* (London: SPCK, 1998).

Stephen Neill, *Anglicanism* (Harmondsworth: Penguin, 1958).

Stephen Platten (ed.), *Anglicanism and the Western Christian Tradition* (Norwich: Canterbury Press, 2003).

Geoffrey Rowell (ed.), *The English Religious Tradition and the Genius of Anglicanism* (Wantage: Ikon, 1992).

Stephen W. Sykes, John Booty, and Jonathan Knight (eds.), *The Study of Anglicanism* (London: SPCK, 1998).

Rowan Williams, *Anglican Identities* (London: DLT, 2004).

William J. Wolf (ed.), *The Spirit of Anglicanism* (Edinburgh: T & T Clark, 1982).

Anglican identity

Paul Avis, *Anglicanism and the Christian Church* (London: T & T Clark, 2002).

Aidan Nichols, *The Panther and the Hind: A Theological History of Anglicanism* (Edinburgh: T & T Clark, 1993).

Colin Podmore, *Aspects of Anglican Identity* (London: Church House Publishing, 2005).

Stephen Sykes, *The Integrity of Anglicanism* (London: Mowbray, 1978).

Stephen Sykes, *Unashamed Anglicanism* (London: DLT, 1995).

Stephen Sykes (ed.), *Authority in the Anglican Communion* (Toronto: Anglican Book Centre, 1987).

Chapter 1

Ian T. Douglas and Kwok Pui-Lan (eds.), *Beyond Colonial Anglicanism* (New York: Church Publishing Inc., 2001).

Robert E. Hood, *Must God Remain Greek? Afro Cultures and God-Talk* (Minneapolis: Fortress Press, 1990).

John S. Mbiti, *Concepts of God in Africa* (London: SCM, 1970).

Chapter 2

John Booty, *John Jewel as Apologist of the Church of England* (London: SPCK, 1963).

Patrick Collinson, *The Religion of the Protestants: The Church in English Society, 1559–1625* (Oxford: Clarendon Press, 1982).

A. G. Dickens, *The English Reformation*, 2nd edn. (London: Batsford, 1988).

Susan Doran and Christopher Durston, *Princes, Pastors and People* (London: Routledge, 2003).

Christopher Haigh, *English Reformations* (Oxford: Clarendon Press, 1993).

Felicity Heal, *Reformation in Britain and Ireland* (Oxford: Oxford University Press, 2003).

Diarmaid MacCulloch, *Thomas Cranmer* (New Haven: Yale University Press, 1995).

Leo F. Stolt, *Church and State in Early Modern England, 1509–1640* (Oxford and New York: Oxford University Press, 1990).

Nigel Voak, *Richard Hooker and Reformed Theology* (Oxford: Clarendon Press, 2003).

Chapter 3

Stephen Collins, *From Divine Cosmos to Sovereign State* (Oxford: Clarendon Press, 1989).

Julian Davies, *The Caroline Captivity of the Church* (Oxford: Clarendon Press, 1992).

Kenneth Fincham, *The Early Stuart Church* (Basingstoke: Macmillan, 1993).

Andrew Foster, *The Church of England 1570–1640* (London: Longman, 1994).

H. R. McAdoo, *The Spirit of Anglicanism* (London: A & C Black, 1965).

Judith Maltby, *Prayer Book and People in Elizabethan and Early Stuart England* (Cambridge: Cambridge University Press, 1998).

John Spurr, *The Restoration Church of England* (New Haven: Yale University Press, 1991).

Nicholas Tyacke, *Anti-Calvinists: The Rise of English Arminianism c.1590–1640* (Oxford: Clarendon Press, 1987).

Peter White, *Predestination, Policy and Polemic* (Cambridge: Cambridge University Press, 1992).

Chapter 4

D. W. Bebbington, *Evangelicalism in Modern Britain* (London: Unwin, 1989).

Colin Buchanan, *Is the Church of England Biblical?* (London: DLT, 1998).

William Gibson, *The Church of England, 1688–1832* (London: Routledge, 2001).

Boyd Hilton, *The Age of Atonement: The Influence of Evangelicalism on Social and Economic Thought* (Oxford: Clarendon Press, 1991).

Kenneth Hylson-Smith, *Evangelicals in the Church of England 1734–1984* (Edinburgh: T & T Clark, 1989).

Alister McGrath, *The Renewal of Anglicanism* (London: SPCK, 1994).

Randle Manwaring, *From Controversy to Co-Existence: Evangelicals in the Church of England* (Cambridge: Cambridge University Press, 1985).

John Martin, *Gospel People? Evangelicals and the Future of Anglicanism* (London: SPCK, 1997).

Ian Randall, *What a Friend We Have in Jesus: The Evangelical Tradition* (London: DLT, 2005).

Nigel Scotland, *Evangelical Anglicans in a Revolutionary Age* (Carlisle: Paternoster, 2004).

Roger Steer, *Church on Fire: The Story of Anglican Evangelicals* (London: Hodder, 1998).

Peter Toon, *Evangelical Theology 1833–1856* (London: Marshall, Morgan and Scott, 1979).

J. Walsh, C. Haydon, and S. Taylor (eds.), *The Church of England, 1689–1833* (Cambridge: Cambridge University Press, 1993).

Chapter 5

James Bentley, *Ritualism and Politics in Victorian Britain: The Attempt to Legislate for Belief* (Oxford: Oxford University Press, 1978).

Yngve Brilioth, *The Anglican Revival: Studies in the Oxford Movement* (London: Longmans, 1925).

Michael Chandler, *An Introduction to the Oxford Movement* (London: SPCK, 2003).

Geoffrey Faber, *Oxford Apostles* (Harmondsworth: Penguin, 1954).

George Herring, *What Was the Oxford Movement?* (London: Continuum, 2002).

Kenneth Hylson-Smith, *High Churchmanship in the Church of England: From the Sixteenth Century to the Late Twentieth Century* (Edinburgh: T & T Clark, 1993).

Francis Penhale, *Catholics in Crisis* (London: Mowbray, 1986).

W. S. F. Pickering, *Anglo-Catholicism: A Study in Religious Ambiguity* (London: SPCK, 1989).

John Shelton Reed, *The Glorious Battle* (Nashville, TN: Vanderbilt University Press, 1996).

Geoffrey Rowell, *The Vision Glorious* (Oxford: Oxford University Press, 1983).

Simon Skinner, *Tractarians and the Condition of England* (Oxford: Clarendon Press, 2004).

Paul Vaiss (ed.), *Newman From Oxford to the People* (Leominster: Gracewing, 1996).

Chapter 6

Alan Acheson, *A History of the Church of Ireland 1691–1996* (Dublin: Columba and APCK, 1997).

Philip Carrington, *The Anglican Church in Canada* (Toronto: Collins, 1963).

Owen Chadwick, *Mackenzie's Grave* (London: Hodder and Stoughton, 1959).

Peter Doll, *Revolution, Religion and National Identity* (Madison: Farleigh Dickinson, 2000).

Curtis Fahey, *In His Name: The Anglican Experience in Upper Canada* (Ottawa: Carleton University Press, 1991).

Jehu Hanciles, *Euthanasia of a Mission* (Westport, CN: Praeger, 2002).

Robert T. Handy, *A History of the Churches in the United States and Canada* (Oxford: Clarendon Press, 1976).

Adrian Hastings, *The Church in Africa, 1450–1950* (Oxford: Clarendon Press, 1994).

Ross Hebb, *The Church of England in Loyalist New Brunswick, 1783–1825* (Madison: Farleigh-Dickinson, 2004).

Peter Hinchliff, *The Anglican Church in South Africa* (London: DLT, 1963).

William Reed Huntington, *The Church-Idea: An Essay Towards Unity* (New York: Scribner's Sons, 1870).

W. M. Jacob, *The Making of the Anglican Church Worldwide* (London: SPCK, 1997).

Bruce Kaye (ed.), *Anglicanism in Australia* (Melbourne: Melbourne University Press, 2002).

Paul V. Marshall, *One Catholic and Apostolic* (New York: Church Publishing, 2004).

Frederick Mills, *Bishops by Ballot* (Oxford: Oxford University Press, 1978).

R. Bruce Mullin, *Episcopal Vision, American Reality* (New Haven: Yale University Press, 1986).

William L. Sachs, *The Transformation of Anglicanism* (Cambridge: Cambridge University Press, 1993).

Alan M. G. Stephenson, *The First Lambeth Conference: 1867* (London: SPCK, 1967).

Alan M. G. Stephenson, *Anglicanism and the Lambeth Conferences* (London: SPCK, 1978).

Bengt Sundkler and Christopher Steed, *A History of the Church in Africa* (Cambridge: Cambridge University Press, 2000).

Richard Vaudry, *Anglicans and the Atlantic World* (Montreal: McGill-Queen's University Press, 2003).

Timothy Yates, *Venn and Victorian Bishops Abroad: The Missionary Policies of Henry Venn* (London: SPCK, 1978).

Chapter 7

Paul Avis, *The Anglican Understanding of the Church* (London: SPCK, 2000).

Ian T. Douglas and Paul F. M. Zahl, *Understanding the Windsor Report* (New York: Church Publishing Inc., 2005).

Matthew Grimley, *Citizenship, Community, and the Church of England: Liberal Anglican Theories of the State Between the Wars* (Oxford: Clarendon Press, 2004).

Robert Hannaford (ed.), *The Future of Anglicanism* (Leominster: Gracewing, 1996).

Andrew Wingate, Kevin Ward, Carrie Pemberton, and Wilson Sitshebo (eds.), *Anglicanism: A Global Communion* (New York: Church Publishing Inc., 1998).

J. Robert Wright (ed.), *Quadrilateral at One Hundred* (London: Mowbray, 1998).

Index

Index

Index

Index

Visit the
VERY SHORT
INTRODUCTIONS
Web site

www.oup.co.uk/vsi

➤ **Information** about all published titles

➤ News of **forthcoming books**

➤ **Extracts** from the books, including titles
  not yet published

➤ **Reviews** and views

➤ **Links** to other **web sites** and main
  OUP web page

➤ Information about **VSIs in translation**

➤ **Contact** the editors

➤ **Order** other **VSIs** on-line